CULT SCARE

A FIRSTHAND ACCOUNT
OF THE
SHOCKING KIDNAPPING
OF KIRSTEN NIELSEN

Copies of this book may be purchased on the web at:

www.cultscare.com

323 East Broadway, Vista, CA 92084
760-631-1833 / 760-631-1880 fax
vista@parchmentpress.net

1st Printing - May 2009
ISBN-13# 978-0-9818641-0-5

CONTENTS

PREFACE

The year was 1976. Kirsten was a rebellious seventeen-year-old Californian who had just run away from home. She hit the road, hitchhiking across the country, looking for love and a place to belong. She found what she was looking for in a community in Chattanooga, Tennessee.

Two years later in 1978, the infamous Jonestown mass suicide happened in Guyana. Mass hysteria and a "cult scare" analogous to the anti-Communist "Red Scare" of the previous generation began springing up everywhere.

In the late '70s, the method used by anti-cultists to "bust cults" was through deprogramming. Several members of the Chattanooga Community were violently seized from the peace of the community only to be harangued, harassed, threatened, and humiliated for adherence to their chosen religious beliefs. The most publicized deprogramming was that of Kirsten Nielsen in 1979, who at the age of 21 and on the day of the wedding of her twin sister, was kidnapped by her parents and associates of Ted Patrick, the notorious Cult Awareness Network deprogrammer.

This is Kirsten's story.

GROWING UP

My name is Kirsten. I had just turned 17 when I first encountered the Community in Chattanooga, Tennessee, in early March of 1976. As a youth I had lived a pretty wild life and had left my parents' home in California as a runaway four or five weeks before I met the Community. I was a desperate, rebellious teenager looking for the answers to life. I hated my parents' comfortable Christian religion and lifestyle. Their outlook on life seemed so shallow, disconnected, and dissatisfying. My mother especially was miserable, and that was proof enough for me. Anyway, I had no desire for a dead, phony, empty religion that couldn't provide me anything of substance. Though I had gone through a boring and frustrating year of catechism, I still didn't have any answers. Coming from a somewhat sheltered childhood, I was beginning to realize that there was a lot of pain in life, and I wanted some real answers.

I was bitter towards my father because I felt cheated by him. He had owned a sound company since about 1945, and it was in the late '60s and '70s when he made it "big" you could say. He and the young men who worked for him — "his boys," as he would call them — set up the P. A. for a lot of the rock-and-roll groups that were just getting started at that time: Joan Baez; Peter, Paul & Mary; Simon & Garfunkel; Bob Dylan; Judy Collins; Jimi Hendrix; Janis Joplin; The Mamas and Papas; Jefferson Airplane (before they became the Starship); the Grateful Dead; James Taylor; Crosby, Stills, Nash & Young; The Who; Country Joe and the Fish, Buffalo Springfield, and many other groups and festivals. I remember seeing in his office some big black and white blow-ups of the Monterey Pop Festival that he did in the late '60s. For a time he did the sound almost weekly for the Filmore West and Winterland in San Francisco, and quite often the Filmore East and countless other places across the US, until Bill Graham, his main competitor, began to take his business away for reasons which I won't go into right now. But during my growing-up years, he was totally consumed with his business and was gone a lot of the time. Yet all along it seemed he was careful to never really let his children know too much of what his business was all about. In fact, he hardly ever talked about it.

So, coming into the frustrating emotional years of youth totally overwhelmed and unprepared to deal with life, I began to discover some thrilling satisfaction and release in drugs and rock-and-roll. Growing up in a permissive home, little restraint and self-control was instilled in me as a young child. Thus, as I grew older, I was easily taken in by peer pressure and other influences around me, and swept away with the spirit of the times, nothing holding me back from the rebellion that was in me. I was fed up with seemingly pointless and empty rules and regulations. I think my mother, seeing the reality of where her children were at, made some sort of a last-ditch attempt to bring us under control, taking it to the extreme. But when you are 12 or 13, it's a little too late, and so her efforts only drove us further apart from her. There was no hope of understanding each other anymore. Reality was that she had already lost us.

I remember hitchhiking to San Francisco to a concert in Candlestick Park one weekend and having the revelation that *this* was our religion. Being there, I felt the closest to life and what it was all about; yet we all went home afterward, just as you do when you go to church. That was really hard. I remember seeing my dad's company truck there, and with a twinge of pain realized more what his business was all about.

Some of my earliest childhood memories were going to folk festivals where my father was doing the sound. These were fond memories for me, but then, as folk turned to rock-and-roll, my father began to hide his business with the music of the times. He sheltered me from this part of America's history. I could have had a front-row seat, but he kept me and my brothers and my sister hidden away from that whole scene and what was going on in Berkeley and Haight-Ashbury at that time.

I'll never forget standing in the sun on Telegraph Avenue in Berkeley one day. Surrounded by all the street merchants, I was filled up with the hope that something new was starting — something from the heart, motivated by the desire for freedom, love, and peace. Beautiful people were everywhere. My heart full of excitement, I started talking with an old hippie about my hope and vision for life. Burnt out and tired, I remember he just looked at me with compassion and said, "Hey, babe, you're about ten years too late." I stood there stunned. His words devastated me. I seemed as one untimely born.

As time passed, I seemed to become aware of so many things, some of which totally overwhelmed me. I became even more resentful towards my father who I felt had sheltered me from the opportunity of a lifetime of growing up in the laps of those who were my only heroes. They were my heroes because they were people who seemed to be more real than anybody else. And somehow I felt that in his heart, my father knew they were real. But being real many times leaves people pretty hopeless, because the reality is that there isn't any hope in the world. That's why Jimi Hendrix and Janis Joplin were dead. But I would rather listen to the prophets of rock-and-roll, who really expressed what was going on in the hearts of the American people, than to the shallow, superficial answers of those who had silenced their inner voice. Those in the leveled mainstream distracted themselves with such things as tennis and church and weekend country clubs, content to avoid the real issues of life.

How could you live with yourself if you didn't know why you were created, where you were coming from, and where you were going? Nothing seemed to make sense to me anymore. Spellbound by the early morning sun glistening off the wet leaves like millions of diamonds, I so often had the sense that life was so precious, and yet how could it be so pointless?

I hated so much the pressure that I felt upon me to just give in and go to school, get a good-paying job, get married, have children, get a nice, little house in suburbia. Then you will be happy, having achieved the so-called ultimate in life, so we were told. It terrified me and made me almost crazy inside. I was filled with so much anger and violence. There had to be something more! If not, I would rather be dead. Janis was right, there was nothing left to lose.

When I was sixteen years old, my mother, out of sheer frustration, gave my aunt custody of me. While I was living with her, my father threw a big party in San Francisco at the Hyatt Regency for "his boys." My sister said she was shocked when she saw him toking on a joint that was being passed around. It was obvious that he loved "his boys" — he was having a great time. Hearing this was really hard for me. Once again, I felt so cheated, so bitter, because he enjoyed what he wouldn't let me in on. It was obvious that the life he was pretending to live and pushing on me had no satisfaction for him either. The poor man apparently had no real answers.

And so ... I liked hanging out with people who couldn't deal with life, because I couldn't either. The thrill of rebellion against a system my parents supported was getting me in a lot of trouble, though. I was in juvenile hall about five or six times during ages 15 and 16. Most of the time it was for being incorrectible (out of control), runaway, and once for possession of alcohol. I was glad they never caught me for the more serious things I was doing. The last time I was in was for about a month, during which I turned 17.

In that time, I remember going to court with my mother — it was clear that my heart was miles and miles away from hers. The verdict was that I was made a ward of the court until I was 18, and would be on probation until I was 21. When I was in juvenile hall this time, I somehow felt so very tired and hopeless. I was at the point where I didn't even want to get out anymore. Maybe it was the best place for me. People who were just like me were there — losers. At least we could relate to each other. Then I got a hold of a couple of books — *One Flew Over the Cuckoo's Nest*, by Ken Kesey, and Tom Wolfe's account of the Merry Pranksters as they drove across the country experimenting with psychedelic drugs in *The Electric Kool-Aid Acid Test*. A new surge for freedom began to fill me. In my mind at the time, my mother was the perfect picture of Nurse Rachet, one of the main characters in *One Flew Over the Cuckoo's Nest*, and all I wanted to do was get out from under her thumb.

After many attempts of negotiating with my probation officer, I was released after finally consenting to the many rules and regulations that my mother had for me. It was made clear to me when I was released that being a ward of the court meant that at any time my mother could call the police to have me picked up, with no explanation needed, since at that point I had been in "Juvy" so many times, was hopelessly rebellious, sometimes violent, and out of control. I think my parents were actually somewhat afraid of me. I remember my father threatening to have me put into a mental institution. Anyway, in this state I just knew I wouldn't endure long, so I packed my bags and kept them in the basement, ready to run at any moment.

A week or two later, my mom called the police on me over a cigarette, so I made a run for it with my younger brother, Peter, who got into trouble for trying to defend me. We stayed two or three weeks in a meadow on the edge of some woods. My brother and I had always been pretty close, but here we came to know and depend on each other even more. We were both so desperate and lost that we couldn't help but cling to one another in the cold winter rain. He was pretty shaken up after just getting back from visiting my twin sister Johanna in Los Angeles for a few weeks.

Johanna had left home a few months before I did, and was now living in Hollywood on Sunset Boulevard with her boyfriend, Pat. She had met him when she was 14 and he was about 24. He was her first sweetheart. She and I used to share a paper route — she did it one day and I the next — and he would come by on his motorcycle and sweep us off our feet, depending on who was doing the paper route that particular day. Neither of us had ever had a boyfriend, much less ever ridden on the back of a motorcycle before, especially hanging onto some guy like this. His skin was so tanned from the hot summer sun. He was one of those really handsome guys, even without his sunglasses on. The attention he gave us was completely irresistible.

But soon it became apparent to me that Johanna was his girl. He preferred her and soon they fell madly in love with one another. I tried to act as if it didn't affect me, but actually inside it hurt a lot, so much that I couldn't really deal with it. So when I was 15, I ran away to Santa Barbara, mainly just to get away from him. "Silver threads and golden needles cannot mend this heart of mine..." Linda Ronstadt was one of his favorites.

Anyway, Pat had a great influence, not only on my sister and me, but on my brothers as well. Life was so exciting with him. He was the one who really turned us on to sex, drugs, and rock 'n' roll. He had a van, and sometimes we would go with him to Berkeley or San Francisco, music blasting out of the window, playing my theme song — "We're not gonna take it, never did and never will!" He was so rebellious and defiant against the system, actually against all authority. With him you felt you could conquer the world. Anything he wanted, he could get. Money wouldn't stop him; he would just steal it. It was really a thrilling occupation. He would teach us exactly how to do it.

I remember us carving swear words in my mother's kitchen table, and my brothers stole her silver and pawned it for drugs and other paraphernalia. My mother was almost having a nervous breakdown over everything, and just left my father and us children for about four or five months. She began to drink and smoke again (something she hadn't done in many years), and see a psychiatrist. She was really desperate.

During this time my father had to go on tour to Philadelphia, so it left us alone for three weeks. Sky was the limit for us. We partied till late in the night, but soon the cabinets became bare. So we decided to stock up again. Pat, our hero, drove us to the grocery store in his van. We had dressed up my younger brother as a woman. We used my mother's wig, her make-up, and her clothes. We were all shocked and very pleased — he looked just like a typical, middle-aged American woman. One of my brother's best friends, Johnny, was going to go with him. How else could I say it except that he was really a cool dude. (Sadly, a few years later, he hung himself in prison, having 22 charges against him for armed robbery. I guess he was really finished. At that time, I don't think any of us had the slightest idea of the devastating consequences of going against our consciences over and over again.)

Anyway, on that day, Johnny, who was about two feet shorter than my brother, was going to act as the son of this woman my brother had become. The excitement was incredible — could we get away with it? They got a shopping cart and went in. Hunger motivated them as they loaded up the cart with steaks, beer, bread, cookies, cola... When the cart was full they headed out through the aisle where there was no cash register. It was so intense — would they be noticed? My brother busily talked to Johnny in a high-pitched voice, trying to act as casual as possible. He had the option of going out the front doors into a large parking lot or making a right and going into an elevator to an upper-level parking lot.

Turning right he walked towards the elevator and pushed the button. Suddenly he heard an employee yelling behind him, "Ma'am! Ma'am! Wait!" Sweat poured down his face. The two stood still. It was too late to make a run for it. The man quickly approached them and said, "Here Ma'am, let me help you with the elevator," holding the door open for him so he could pass through. My brother cordially thanked him in his high-pitched voice, calling little Johnny into the elevator. The man smiled and walked away. The doors closed. My brother Peter and Johnny, laughing together, almost fainted with relief. It was too much...

The rest of us waited in the van, tensely watching the elevator door. Would he make it? What would happen? Suddenly, the doors opened and Peter and Johnny rolled out, the cart full to the brim. We could hardly contain our joy. What a victory it seemed, yet we were so unaware of the fact that we were setting the course of our eternal destiny, and that every man will render an account for every deed he's done, for or against his conscience.

Well, the cabinets were full again, and the music continued until late in the night. Life seemed good until one morning we woke up to the sound of walkie-talkies. Crashed out on the living-room floor, we all laid around with wine bottles and drug paraphernalia everywhere. The place was a wreck. Our friends were all gone. My head aching from a hangover, I could hear my father's voice, "Here's one over here, and here's another one over there." One by one, we were pulled to our feet and handcuffed and escorted to the police car. As I was being taken out of the house, I suddenly became aware that the other policemen in the house seemed kind of nervous. I could hear my father by the bathroom, saying, "Here! It seems he got out the window." The policemen began running around everywhere, searching the house and the yard. I got it that they couldn't find Peter. I was happy. At least one of us got away. The three of us were off to juvenile hall again — a large, heavily guarded compound with high security.

I was such a loser in every area, and actually so worthless about it that I took my identity in being as bad as possible. I think it was pretty much this way with all of us children. By the time my older brother was eleven, he was doing morphine, stole $200 worth of records with my other brother, and got caught for stealing a car and possession of uppers.

Anyway, it was with this man Pat that my sister went to Hollywood. He always seemed to be going through different phases. Over the previous year, he was getting more and more into dressing in "drag." He was taking a walk on the wild side with Lou Reed, getting a real thrill out of looking like a woman. He would steal very seductive, flashy-looking clothes with my sister from Frederick's of Hollywood and other places. He let his hair grow even longer, and with lots of make-up on, he looked like a very "pretty" hooker. So in Hollywood he and my sister both prostituted, but especially her. He mostly had her making the money. And when she wasn't prostituting, she worked as a dancer in a night club. Over these months he became more and more violent. I guess he always was, but especially now, according to what my brother was telling me about his visit down there. He said my sister was getting beat up all the time and that this guy would kick her mercilessly with his steel-toed boots. He broke her finger, put her head through a plate glass window, and threw her out of the apartment in the middle of the night with no clothes on. He was really treating her bad. They were both sniffing a lot of cocaine and mainlining heroin at this time. It made my brother and me really sad.

LEAVING CALIFORNIA

While I was camping out in the meadow, I reflected on a lot of things and decided to leave California for good. I wanted to get as far away as possible. Actually, I guess I was running from a lot of things. After sadly parting with my brother who decided to turn himself in, and with only $4.50 on me, I started hitchhiking up the northern coastline through Mendocino County on Highway 1. Then I crossed over through Oregon and headed toward New York City. I figured this was the farthest place I could go.

Before I left, I confided in a woman who lived down the street and whom I had known for a long time. Then, during our time together in the meadow, whenever my brother and I would come to her house, she would always feed us and give me a listening ear. Even though her husband was a probation officer, they never thought to turn us in. She had four children herself and seemed to have a lot of understanding and compassion. She was a friend to me. She didn't push herself on me, pretending to have all the answers, yet she was there when I needed her. Somehow I could trust her. I knew that she was for me. Anyway, when I told her about my plans to leave for New York in a few days, I could tell she was a little worried and concerned about me. She showed me a newspaper clipping with a picture of her brother and his wife, who ran a delicatessen in Chattanooga, Tennessee. She said they took people in, and if I needed a place to stay on my way to New York, I surely could stay there for a while. After she told me this, I set my heart on Tennessee as a sure resting place before continuing to New York.

After a hard four or five weeks on the road, I finally made it to Chattanooga, Tennessee. A man who picked me up in Oregon told me that 90% of the girls that hitchhike in the US are either murdered or raped. I don't know if this is true or not. Nevertheless, I believe it was nothing short of a miracle — I mean something to do with God and with angels — that I even made it to Tennessee.

One time along the way I got into some trouble with the police in a little town in Arkansas. I remember I ended up at a small truck stop near Little Rock. Two truckers laughing their head off, threw a few dollars at me out their window for lending my female services. They scared me a little, as they seemed like the kind that had little scruples left about life. So I cooperated and made it out alive, with a few more dollars for another meal. I guess that was life for a "beaver" out in the Midwest. Anyway, reflecting on my last weeks over a cup of coffee in this redneck truck stop, I debated whether I should order a piece of banana cream pie. It seemed

I would have had enough money, but just one thing was really bothering me. Sitting several tables away from me was a very strange-looking man with evil-looking eyes. For five minutes I noticed he hadn't stopped staring at me. I was getting really bad vibes from him, and I wondered if I should just get up and walk out. Just then the waitress came and asked if I wanted anything else. I hesitated, but then just went ahead and ordered the pie. In the meantime, as I waited for my order, the man walked out. "Ah, evil is past!" I thought.

Sitting there enjoying my pie, I looked up, and to my great alarm, that same man was coming in the door, walking straight towards my table followed close behind by a police officer. "Surely they will walk past my table. They can't be coming for me," I thought. I hadn't done anything wrong! My mind was racing, trying to think what name I would tell them and how old I would say I was. Then what I feared happened. They stopped right besides me. As I looked up at the policeman, he gruffly and very authoritatively asked, "What's your name?"

"Connie," I said.

"Connie what!?" he barked.

"Connie Kristen."

"How old are you?"

"Twenty two," I said.

"Okay, look, we know you put your bags in the women's room and we're gonna go with you and you're going to get them. And if you try to jump out the window, we're gonna be on you like flies on a jam jar!"

It seemed this was an original southern redneck police officer. Feeling defeated and out of strength, I went and got my bags, with one of them on either side. I couldn't believe I had made it thus far only to get caught for nothing in some Podunk town.

Out by the police car, the two talked together for a few minutes, and then the strange man left. He was probably some kind of bored narc who had nothing to do that afternoon. The police officer then put me in the back of his car and began to talk to me, looking at me through his rearview mirror.

"I'm going to ask you again what your name is, and if you don't tell me what your real name is you're gonna sit in jail until you rot."

Later on, I found out that the law is that if you didn't do anything wrong and if they don't have any information on you, they have to let you go after three days. Leaning my head against the window, the tears began to roll down my face. It was all so pointless. I had almost made it to Chattanooga. I gave up all resistance and for the first time cooperated with a police officer.

I told him my real name and age and where I was from. Doing some communications on his radio, he asked how long I had been traveling. I said about five weeks. He was surprised, and after this point, somehow his heart seemed to change towards me. He asked kindly if I had any trouble along the way. I said no. He told me they had no jail for juveniles in this town, only an adult jail which he would have to put me in. Then he said compassionately that he was going to get me the best probation officer they had.

I couldn't believe how nice he was. Something had changed in him and I didn't know why. Still, I was pretty down because I knew when my parents found out where I was, they'd never let me see the light of day for a long time. I could see myself ending up in some girl's detention home in the backwoods of Arkansas, only to get in one kind of trouble after the other... I was so tired.

A few minutes later, I found myself standing in front of a metal grill covered window, answering questions again. As I bent down to open my bags to be searched, the policeman who had brought me there kicked my bags across the room before I could touch them. It struck me a little strange the way he did it, not in anger, but rather slyly. The whole time his face remained looking at the woman on the other side of the grill. I had hash pipes in my bag and I had heard that if they really want to get you for something, they can bust you for the resin and the pipes. Maybe he was trying to spare me.

Then I found myself talking to another woman — the best probation officer they had. She seemed very nice as she informed me what the law was. She said she would have to inform my parents about where I was. If they did not respond within three days, letting her know what they wanted to do with me, they would have to let me go.

Once alone in my cell, I stared out the bare window. I couldn't see anything because it was smoked glass, but I could get the sunlight as it dully shone on the jail-green walls. Well, here I was again, feeling so hopeless and at the end, knowing that it was impossible that my parents would ever release me. I began to whisper a prayer. "God, if you are real, then please, please help me, and get me out of here." I promised to give Him my life if He would get me out of there. I earnestly prayed this over and over again for three days. And so I waited... On the third day, my probation officer came.

"Do you want a ride out to the interstate?" she asked.

I could hardly believe it! "Did I hear right?! What?" I said, trying to contain myself.

"Well, your parents never called, so by law we have to let you go. Do you want a ride to the interstate?" she asked again with a smile.

"Sure!"

As we drove, she warned me about no hitchhiking in Arkansas, but she said that if you just stand on the side of the highway the truckers will pick you up. I knew she was right about that one. Her only other concern seemed to be about birth control. Anyway, after talking about that subject for a few minutes, I got out of the car and thanked her, and we said good-bye.

There I was — a free woman, standing on the side of the road again. Maybe I'll get to New York after all, but first Chattanooga. My thoughts were quickly interrupted as a truck stopped to pick me up. Years later, I found out that the woman had told my father five days rather than three. My mother told me that my father was so angry when he called on the fifth day to tell them what to do with me. (By the way, I never did find out what was on their mind...)

Next it was Kansas. My sleeping bag had been stolen by a trucker who took advantage of me. It was dark. I was alone. It was still winter and I was cold and tired. If I only had my sleeping bag I could sleep somewhere off the side of the road, but it was in some truck headed east. The man had said he would wait for me while I took a shower, but he didn't. I was stupid. Seventeen and not feeling a day wiser, I walked down the road, cars whizzing by. I saw lights from a building on the left-hand side. A sign out front read, "The Church of the Nazarene." Maybe I could get some help there, I thought.

It was Wednesday night and they were having their little get-together. The room was dark because the people were watching a film strip. Jesus wore a bright white robe. His face kind of glowed and his feet seemed to hardly touch the ground. Women seemed insignificant and only able to cry. Watching for a few minutes, my liberal Californian feminism was insulted. Fortunately the projector broke. The lights went on. Now was my chance. I walked to the man fixing the tape.

"Excuse me. Do you know of anyone who could help me? Maybe a place to stay the night and something to eat?"

The man (I assumed it was the pastor) seemed unprepared for the question. He looked carefully out over his congregation. Slowly he looked over everyone from one side of the room to the other. I had caught several people's attention by now. I saw a woman draw her children close. She seemed a little disgusted and afraid of me. Suddenly the room began to feel cold, the pews orderly and hard. The man looked back at me. "No, I'm sorry," he stammered, "I don't know of anyone who can help you."

A little stunned, I turned around. Out in the cold again, I continued on down the busy road wondering why the people who claimed to know God were like that. Was God like that? If He was, I determined that I didn't want to know Him. After another couple of blocks, I saw another tall, religious building on the right-hand side. I thought I would try again. It looked more fancy, though, with a big glass door in the front. A small light was burning from somewhere inside, and the door was open. Carefully walking in, I followed the light leading me down a short hallway and into a room where a woman and two men were speaking. She was an older, orderly looking woman with short hair and black modest-heeled shoes. One of the men had a high black collar — obviously the pastor or priest. They all looked at me in surprise.

Feeling very out of place, I asked, "Do you know of anyone who could help me? I'm traveling and I would need a place for the night."

They looked at each other and then decided, "No," they didn't know of anyone, but if I would go way down to the end of the street, maybe the Catholic Church could help me.

Once again, the cold night air hit my cheeks. This was too much. I couldn't understand Christians. Actually, I had always known them to be this way — hypocrites, fake, phony, cold, orderly, and dead. On I went. After a while I began to hear singing. It was coming from a rather humble, small-looking, red brick building on the left-hand side. I almost felt drawn as I walked over to it and up the stairs to the door. People seemed alive inside. A man began to speak with some passion, and the people actually responded. I had never seen this before. I walked to the front bench. Everything the pastor said made me cry. I pinched my hand so hard, trying not to, but I couldn't stop. I felt so tired and finished. What was the purpose to my life? Why was I created? I wanted to believe him that there was a God who cared.

The congregation seemed to break up a little. Suddenly there was a young girl beside me. She seemed so sweet. Very kindly, she asked me whether I knew Jesus. Sitting there crying, I shook my head, "No."

She said, "Do you want to know Him?"

I said, "No."

She wasn't offended, and her presence seemed comforting. She asked me whether I had a place to stay for the night.

I said, "No."

She told me that the man who had been speaking was her father, and said for sure I could come home with them. She brought me to her father, who seemed warm and nice. Without hesitating, he said surely I could come home with them.

After going downstairs for about twenty minutes for a kind of strange time of cake and coffee, this girl, her parents, five other younger brothers and sisters, and I all piled into a big car and went to their house. Here they gave me a nice bed in the same room with that 19-year-old girl whose name I do not remember.

In the morning, before the girl was going to take me to the interstate, I passed through her father's study. He stopped me and talked to me for a few minutes about Jesus. I don't remember all that he said, but I could tell he was concerned about me.

At the end, he very seriously asked me if I wanted to know Jesus.

Afraid, I said, "No," looking down.

He said, "Well, if you are ever in any trouble and you need help, here's my card with my number on it. You can call me any time."

His love touched my heart. After that, I got in their big red truck, and the girl drove me to the highway. I said good-bye and right before I got out the girl began to cry. She took a small wooden cross from around her neck and put it around mine. She said she would pray for me. I believe she will be remembered for what she did for me.

After she drove off, I stood there and cried. I felt so confused, maybe God was real. Maybe He did care about me. I took a chance and prayed with all of my heart that if He was real that He would please reveal Himself to me.

I continued heading down the road. My last ride into Chattanooga was with a man who got stopped by the police on the interstate just before a turn-off. I didn't know why they stopped him. They were asking him a lot of questions. I was nervous. I didn't want to make it this far and get caught. I opened the door slowly, slipped out, and began to walk down the interstate. I jumped over the guardrail and disappeared down the embankment. I couldn't believe I had made it out of that one. At the bottom of the hill was a big fence with barbed wire all along the top. I threw my coat and my last bag over, but couldn't get over myself. I had to find another way out. Coming out a few blocks over, a businessman in a big fancy car asked me if I needed some help. I said yes and got in. After driving around for a while, I found my bags. He kindly let me out. Somehow, I was always amazed that I still had my life after encounters like that. On the road you never know what people's real motives are. Maybe they are good, maybe they are bad.

Anyway, now here I found myself, down at the railroad yard. It was kind of a lonely place, and it was beginning to rain. I walked around and saw some shacks on the left, but kept walking past an old wooden church. I stood there looking for a moment, wondering if I could spend the night in there. It would be out of the rain, but the doors were locked shut as usual.

A car pulled up and a young black man called out to me, "Hey, whacha lookin' for?"

I said, "Some food and a place to stay."

He said, "Get in."

I got in, and he drove in a circle through the mud until we got back to the first shack. He said kindly, "My mama saw you out the winda and told me to come get you."

I could hardly believe it was true. We got out and went up some old wooden stairs. At the top stood an old black woman. She said, "Come on in, honey. Get yourself in out of all that rain." She really took care of me, giving me some dry clothes, the last two hot dogs in the pot, and a couch to sleep on. She was so kind.

That evening we sat around, talking a little bit with her daughter and her older son. She had two or three little grandchildren running around. I told her I was looking for a delicatessen that was run by a couple that took people in. She said I could use her phone and the phone book to try to find it.

Since I didn't have the phone number, I took a guess. The first delicatessen I called was a place named *Shapiros*. They told me I was looking for the *Yellow Deli* on Brainard Road. They gave me the number, and I called this place. They were really friendly and even said they could come and get me that night. I told them no, I would find my way in the morning. So I spent the night there and started to head over the next morning.

The black woman insisted on bringing me over. She told me I'd have to go through 9th Street to get there, and 9th Street, she said, was really dangerous. Someone like me wouldn't come out the same, she said, telling me she'd take me over in a little while. I thought she was totally anxious, so when she turned her head I tried to slip out the door. She was after me in a flash, grabbing the youngest child in her arms. She said, "Come on, honey, I'll take you over right now. You can't walk through 9th Street!" I believe God will remember this lady in the Judgment for all her care.

MEETING THE COMMUNITY

CHATTANOOGA, TENNESSEE

At the *Yellow Deli* I was met by very kind people. As soon as I walked in, I felt different. "Welcome" is the only word to describe it. It was so warm and so real. The people were natural, friendly, relaxed — just plain normal. They had peace. After spending a short time there in the *Yellow Deli*, someone brought me over to the place where the single women lived in one of their several Community houses on Vine Street. My first encounter with the young women there intrigued me. They seemed to have so much dignity and purpose, and at the same time they were very cheerful and hospitable in a genuine way. I admired them. They seemed so different. One women showed me my bunk and told me that I could get settled in, and that supper would be at the house on the corner, called *The Vine House*, at 6 o'clock. They left and I was alone. From the moment I met these people, I kind of felt as if I was in a dream. I sat down on the floor and looked out the window, my chin resting on the window sill. The feeling of the old south drifted in on the afternoon breeze, moving the shear curtains. The old houses lay under the canopy of the ancient elm and oak trees, their gnarly roots buckling the sidewalk. "Where have I landed," I wondered? Everything seemed so peaceful as I watched a dove land on the neighbor's roof.

At six o'clock, I cautiously made my way over to the Vine House. I could hear singing coming from the open windows. When I walked into the door I was stunned to see about fifty or sixty people around one long table. Like one big happy family, they were singing and having a good time. Somehow it didn't register to me that they were singing about God. They all had long hair and beards, and were much too happy and friendly to be Christians. As I came to find out more about them, the amazing thing was that they never went home. They *were* home. They lived and worked together. I could see that they had a real friendship between them, relating to each other with love and affection, yet not in an exclusive way. It was unlike anything I had ever seen. So in the days that followed, I found myself falling in love with them more and more. I was drawn to the God they knew. I wanted to have what they had, and to know their God. Actually, I was jealous because deep down inside, I'd always desired to be part of a true brotherhood, a place to belong, and here I found it — and what's more, it was being offered to me.

A few days passed, until one sunny Sunday afternoon, I remember sitting on a bench in a rose garden at a local park. It was after one of their gatherings. I was profoundly affected. It was so unlike anything that I had ever experienced or associated with going to church. It seemed so normal and relaxed how they all sat in a circle in the grass, children and all. There was nothing weird, stale or musty about it. Even when they spoke it wasn't monotonous, boring, and removed. They would stand up randomly as they felt moved and speak to each other in a very sincere way, sometimes passionately, really something from their heart. I didn't understand all they were saying, but it made me cry. I somehow felt God was there, and that somehow He was near to me.

Anyway, after the gathering they were all starting to go back to the communal houses, and I was sitting there pretty much alone, contemplating my life and the things I was seeing and hearing, when one of the men came over to me. Despite the picture of dejection that I was he hugged me warmly and looked me straight in the eye. With the most heartfelt sincerity, which I will never forget, he told me that God really loved me. He then walked away, joining his wonderful wife with her beautiful warm smile. Both of them were waving good-bye to me in the afternoon sun, radiating so much love, I felt I was looking at angels. It was the very first time in my life that I dared to believe that God really did exist, and that He loved me, although I had been told many times before, "The Lord loves you." I remembered a few days before, on that lonely day in Kansas, standing on the side of the road and praying with all of my heart that if God was real that He would reveal Himself to me and show me where He was! Is that what was happening now? Could it be? I couldn't hold back the tears. I sat there crying for a long, long time, overwhelmed with the feeling that I had finally come home.

In the days that passed, faith grew more and more in me that this God was the very same One who created the most amazing sunrises and sunsets, the One who created everything — even me. After such a frantic and desperate search, I finally knew the purpose for which I had been created. I was no longer an accident, a misfit, wishing I'd never been born.

Yet with the growing awareness of His love for me also came the awareness of how guilty I was. In the midst of these clean people I felt so dirty. Even though I was only 17, reality was that my sins had already piled up so high. I knew there was no way I could ever pay for all my rebellion and the pain I had caused others. The self-destructive path I was headed down was leaving a wake behind me, leading me to eternal death. My childhood innocence was gone, and I had made such a mess of my life. I so much wished I could start all over again with a clean slate.

I believed God had the power to forgive me of all my deep, deep guilt. I desired so much to have a clean conscience, and to give my life to this God whose love I'd experienced in such a real way. I believed He loved me so much that He provided a sacrifice that could cover my sins and give me this chance of a new start. So after a few months in the Community in Chattanooga, I was baptized into His Son for the forgiveness of my sins. I never wanted to leave Him or His people. This was the beginning of my life as a true disciple of the Son of God.

Soon I communicated to my parents the excitement of my new life, of what had happened to me. The last they knew, I was in jail in Little Rock. They seemed very happy, and right away sent a letter giving Gene and Marsha Spriggs (this couple who started the Community, and who had especially befriended me) guardianship of me until I was 18, in case there was any trouble with the authorities. (Gene was the brother of the neighbor woman in California whom I mentioned confiding in earlier. It all came back to us, after being around each other for a few days, that we had already met in his sister's house in California when I was about fifteen or sixteen. Even though the encounter had been brief, it was outstanding to me how kind they had been. It was pretty amazing how it all came together.) Anyway my parents were so relieved that I was safe and out of trouble, and better yet, in a place that was God-orientated.

MY SISTER JOINS THE COMMUNITY

Ever since I had become a part of the Community, I couldn't stop thinking about my twin sister. I wanted her to come and experience the new life I'd found. I knew she had to be totally miserable just as I had been. I felt so bad for her. Eventually I got in touch with her and begged her to come and see me. Finally it happened in June or July of that same year. Her boyfriend Pat was so possessive of her. She had to leave without him knowing about it, because he would never have let her go. It was an intense chase all the way. He, of course, noticed right away that she was gone. He knew that she had called me at one point, so he called me desperately looking for her. I tried to be vague and said that I didn't really know whether she was coming to see me or not.

Feeling uneasy about the situation, the elders of the Community moved my sister and me to the private house of a friend. Pat had phoned and said he would be about three days in coming. Of course, he lied and arrived in about half the time in one of our *Yellow Delis* in Trenton, Georgia, where he thought she might be, looking for her frantically. He came with his big dog and that boy Johnny. He was almost insane from lack of sleep, doing speed all the way from California. He aggressively demanded that we give her to him.

Safely away at that friend's house, I talked to her incessantly. I was so happy with my new life and I wanted her to be set free from her miserable condition and have what I had — a fresh new start, a new beginning, a place to belong where love was our home, filled with real brothers and sisters. That is what we had always wanted to be and to have — a place to receive healing from all the things we had gone through. Deep down in my heart, it was everything I ever desired, and I just knew it must be her desire, too. But unfortunately, it really wasn't. As miserable as her life was, she didn't want to let go of it. It became evident to me after the first few days of her visit that she was not ready to give up her life for this life. She only wanted a break, a rest from the intensity of things, and so all my talking wasn't good news to her as it was to me. She just wanted me to go to the next *Rolling Stones* concert with her in Candlestick Park.

However unrelenting, I continued to talk to her, hoping she would see what I saw. Finally, she decided to stay. Her suppressed conscience was awakened through the things I told her, and it condemned her for the life she was living and for the things she gave herself to. So when she assented to stay, it was out of guilt from a bad conscience. And of course, there was an emotional bond that's probably especially strong between us as identical twins. She came into the Community for different reasons than I did. However, it took years until I completely understood this. It was not because she loved the life here and hated her own life and wanted to be delivered from it. So the salvation that I had found, that transferred me from my old life into this new life in the Community, had no real appeal to her.

I guess when it comes right down to it, she really loved her life. If her conscience hadn't been reproving her for it, making her feel guilty, she wouldn't have had a problem continuing to indulge in the things she gave herself to. Sad to say, but I think her state was that she only wanted to be delivered from the judgment *for* her sins, but not *from* her sins — the cause of judgment in the first place. But the Savior that we in the Community came to know didn't just come to deliver us from the judgment of our sins by merely forgiving us for our selfish ways. He came to actually *save* us from these sins, by being immersed into this amazing life in the Community, where we don't need to live for ourselves anymore, but are really set free to take care of each other. He made it very clear that you have to hate your life in this world if you want to follow Him and experience His salvation. I had never seen or even heard of a place where the words of the Bible were being lived out. I had never seen such love before as in the Community.

Later on, my sister went on to find a god according to her liking. But while she was in the Community, she was, in a sense, like a slave, the desire to leave always working in her. And of course she was always free to go. But whenever she came close to packing her bags and hitting the road, I would always talk her into staying because of my emotional love for her. This, along with the condemnation of her guilty conscience, always held her. I honestly wanted the best for her, and I don't know what would have become of her life had she not come to see me at that time. So many times in life, you know what would have been better afterwards. Now I understand that you can't talk people into doing what you know is the best for them if it's not really in their heart to do it.

MY PARENTS

For the next year and a half I continued to write to my parents, and once again, in hindsight, I can see that I lacked wisdom in my letters. As a teenager, I really hated their comfortable Christian religion and lifestyle, and was so happy when I came to the Community and saw a real life and real love behind the words of people who professed to know God. So in my over-zealous, dogmatic letters, there was still an element of rebellion working in me towards them to just want to prove a point, just how wrong their religion and lifestyle was.

To make things worse, my sister's communications with them probably revealed her discontentment and unhappiness. At times she was very emotional with them on the phone. Unknown to me, a seed of fear about the Community began to grow in my parents. My mother got in touch with anti-cult organizations in Berkeley and throughout the Bay Area — the "Freedom Foundation," which later became the "Cult Awareness Network," and the "Spiritual Counterfeits

Project," etc. So this was the stage prior to my parents' first visit to the Community in 1977.

My parents had planned on staying two weeks. But my father had to leave after a few days to do business in Philadelphia, only returning for the last few days before they flew back to California. My mother was very uneasy, nervous, and emotional when she came. It was obvious during their stay that she already had her mind made up about the Community, and the visit was only to confirm her fears. She seemed to always read something between the lines, frantically taking notes in a suspicious, negative way about everything people said. It became clear during this first visit that their initial positive attitude toward us being part of the Chattanooga Community had really changed for the worse. For the next two and a half years, it seems she only became more and more convinced about the Community being a cult, as she continued to gather misinformation about us.

In November 1979, I called my parents and told them I was going to get married on the 25th of December to someone I had become very close to, and had known since I first arrived in Chattanooga. At the same time, a similar situation had been going on with my sister, who was living in another community. Our relationships with our fiancés were in somewhat different stages, and probably we would have naturally gotten married three or four months apart, but out of courtesy for my parents it was decided to have our weddings almost at the same time so that they wouldn't have to make two flights from California only a few months apart. They seemed happy for us and said that certainly they would come.

Another thing that really played on my mother's emotions and actually triggered her final decision to take action was a letter from her sister who was staying together with her husband in France, where he was working on a scientific project for the US government. At the beginning of this letter she wrote, "Joyce, I had a dream, actually more of a vision, last night, and in the vision your daughter Kirsten was screaming, 'Help me!! Help me!! Mama! Mama! Help me!! Help me!!!' I don't know what it means, but I thought I would tell you." My mother took this as a sign.

Kidnapping, the beginning of deprogramming

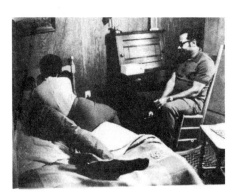

Ted Patrick in a deprogramming session

THE KIDNAPPING

DECEMBER, 1979

The day I expected my parents would fly into Chattanooga we heard nothing from them. It seemed unusual, but I thought maybe they were just tired from the trip and would call the next day. I heard nothing for two more days. This was beginning to seem strange to me. I called my grandmother. She was surprised and said they should have arrived three days ago. She didn't know what happened.

The lack of peace my parents had about me and my sister being here was obvious through different comments they had made over the years, and so we didn't trust their intentions. Old fears began to come to me, considering how they used to call the police without warning on us as children before. My sister and I began to suspect the possibility of them getting in touch with Ted Patrick, a deprogrammer who was becoming sort of infamous at the time. "Black Lightning" was the name he had acquired, for the simple fact that he was a black man who would swoop in like lightning and kidnap people from various so-called "cults." It seemed highly possible that they had hired this man and had now spent the past three days conspiring together, planning to kidnap and deprogram us. I expressed all my fears to some of my friends. And even though our community had already experienced some deprogrammings in the past, it was still hard for them to imagine someone doing such an outrageous thing. Nevertheless, they advised us not to go anywhere with our family alone, or at least not without our fiancés with us.

On the third day they finally called. My mother sounded very happy and at peace. She said she was sorry for the delay, but they had wanted to rest up for a few days before coming as the trip had been a little hard on my father. She assured us that Dad and she, as well as my two younger brothers who had come along for the occasion couldn't wait to see me and my sister. I was so excited, as I hadn't seen my brothers for almost four years. The way she said it sounded all so reasonable and I began to feel a little stupid for ever suspecting them of planning such a ridiculous thing as kidnapping us.

When they arrived at some of the community houses on Vine Street, they appeared very much at ease. None of them seemed at all nervous or out of character, only happy and genuinely glad to see us. I didn't sense any anxiety. My brothers had changed a lot. I hardly recognized them with their mustaches. They were so tall. I left them as boys and now they were young men, 18 and 19, towering over me. It was a happy reunion, and I felt so awful for ever thinking they were up to something. Every fear of mine vanished in the morning sunshine, and I even felt a twinge of regret that I had thought such things.

I had to laugh when I saw they had rented a silver Mercedes. My dad only got the best.

They expressed how they had really not had time to buy something for my sister and me, and although they knew my sister's wedding was only two hours away, they wondered if there was any way we could go with them and do a little quick shopping. They had also expressed how they really wanted to get something for us they knew we'd really need and enjoy. Of course, they didn't want to make her late for her wedding, but there must be a mall around here somewhere. My mother was very convincing and at the same time didn't seem to be pressuring us. It all seemed so innocent, something we'd do almost more for her sake than ours. You almost hated to disappoint her. My sister and I told her fiancé and another friend of ours that we had obviously misjudged them. They just wanted to take us shopping for a little bit, and we'd be back shortly. Everything was all right and we didn't really need anybody to go with us. I remembered how with worried faces they watched us go.

Happily, my sister and I got in the back seat with our two brothers on either side. At the mall, my father and brothers quickly disappeared. We wondered where they went. My mother said with a smile, "You know how they hate shopping."

"Oh yes, of course," I thought.

"They've probably gone to find something of interest in the Hi-Fi and TV department, or the hardware section," she continued.

After having gotten a pair of shoes and a jacket for me, and a leather handbag for my sister, the men finally reappeared and we were ready to go. By then, time was really running out. Quickly, we hurried out to the car. It was a large parking lot with many cars continually pulling in and out. We didn't think anything about this car that had pulled out right in front of us. And so as we headed back toward the Community, we were completely unaware that we were actually continually following behind this particular car...

My sister was past being nervous and was now depressed. Her smile was gone. There was so little time left, and she still needed to take a bath and get ready for her wedding. She noticed that we seemed to be going the wrong way and said something about it. My dad didn't answer. I looked at him. His face was red and I thought he was probably embarrassed because my dad never loses his way — he has an excellent sense of direction, even if he'd never been there before. He'll find his way, I thought, not a bit afraid or suspicious as my mother rattled on cheerfully.

"Honey, show Dad your new shoes and jacket. Look Don, isn't it nice?" She successfully distracted us. I should say me — my sister was pretty bummed out. Her smile never returned. She knew she probably wouldn't make it on time anymore...

Suddenly the car took a sharp right, sped up a long steep private driveway, and abruptly parked in the back of a green house that I had never seen before. In an instant, the doors flew open and my brothers, who were on either side of my sister and me, quickly got out and stood blocking the open car doors. In the same moment, my father was out of the car in a flash, and walked quickly to the back door of the house as six or seven people came out to meet him. One of them, a very overweight, older-looking man, walked directly to my father. They shook hands — it was obvious this was a business deal.

This is always a horrible moment for me to remember. It was definitely a traumatic experience. All my worst fears from a few days before suddenly became a horrifying reality. It was like a nightmare. My sister and I looked at each other in total shock and began to moan. "It's Ted Patrick! We're being deprogrammed!!" My mind was frantically looking for a way out, but there was no escape. It was hopeless. My brothers who were guarding the doors were six feet tall, young and athletic. We didn't stand a chance. My mother slowly turned around in the front seat. She didn't say anything. There was a tear on her cheek, yet what also seemed to me a familiar look of triumph. I felt so betrayed.

THE DEPROGRAMMING

The people near the house had now come and stood around the car. We were told to get out. They surrounded us and we were escorted through the back door and into a living room. No one talked to us. They only talked quietly to each other. Then they left us for a few minutes alone with my mother on the couch. My sister and I sat in silence and unbelief at what was happening. Suddenly, a young woman named Melinda Horton appeared, hair cropped and face covered with make-up. What happened?! I almost didn't recognize her. Although I hadn't seen her in more than three years, I remembered her quite well as a completely different person from the time she lived with us in the Community. This was the girl who had disappeared from our midst in summer 1976. Her parents had kidnapped her and had her deprogrammed by Ted Patrick. That's all we knew. This was the first time we had anything to do with that sort of stuff. And although we had tried to find out more, as we loved and cared about her and thought that was how she felt about us too, no one had been able to. All our efforts in contacting her were thwarted. It was all so mysterious.

But now here she was, explaining to my sister and me that we were going to be deprogrammed by Ted Patrick and his team who she'd become a part of. Having joined the deprogrammers, she was now a zealot for the cause. Talk about changing camps! My mind could hardly make the switch. Sitting there with her hair cut and her face full of make-up, she so sweetly told us that after it was all over we would, of course, be free to go back. "But you probably won't want to." Listening to her made me sick. I could hardly believe she was for real. We were told that the deprogramming would begin right away, but Ted wouldn't arrive due to circumstances until three days later. We would be forced to remain here until the deprogramming was over, which could be indefinite, so they said. My sister and I were then led into separate rooms. It was the last time I saw her until it was all over, three or four days later.

So now here I was, sitting in this room with the doors locked and people all around guarding me so that I couldn't get away. If I needed to use the restroom, I was escorted so that I wouldn't jump out of the window. Then began the grueling ordeal. Lies and accusations about the Community were continuously being spoken to me. The leaders and our beliefs were constantly being torn down and slandered. False documents and pictures were presented or promised to be. It was very exasperating. No Bible or private time was given to us except to sleep. Any form of prayer, meditation, or singing was immediately interrupted by either many words, loud piano music, or any other means they could find. There was really no escape from the barrage of their "mind-control" propaganda. Two or three of them would be aggressively talking to me at the same time. When one didn't know what to say, the other one did. If you said anything contrary they constantly came back at you. It was very exasperating and exhausting.

What these deprogrammers wanted was that my mind would be open, listening, and focused on what they were saying, persistently trying to find an inroad, a crack in the wall that would undermine the supposed "programming." Through Margaret Singer, a well-known psychiatrist from Berkeley, California, Ted Patrick had learned some about deprogramming because of her work with the American prisoners of war that were said to have been put under mind control during the Korean War. The extent of his relationship with her and how much exactly he learned from her I don't really know. Their theory was that if a person had been programmed in the first place, he could be deprogrammed.

One of the things I have learned through all of this and am convinced of is that you cannot deprogram revelation that comes from the Holy Spirit. If you really have heard God speak to you in your heart — and this is what faith is — that can never be taken away from you, because faith is not a program. It's something that has to do with the heart of God and with the heart of man. It goes beyond some kind of brain thing. Yet besides my own personal convictions about this, it's even been proven that the brainwashing theory is scientifically unsound.[1]

Anyway, this whole deprogramming thing was so ridiculously ironic because their way of thinking and viewing the Community was being so violently forced upon me unlike anything I had ever experienced in my whole life. I say "violently" not in the respect of having been beaten, but in that it was such a stark violation of my will.

I found out later that my sister had tried to jump out the bathroom window. I don't know what story she gave them, but somehow she made it to go to the bathroom herself and have the woman who was watching her wait outside the door. Once inside, she quickly opened the window and climbed up onto the sink. She barely had pulled herself up and was getting ready to jump when the door burst open and several people, having heard some strange noises, rushed in and grabbed her by her shirt just a fraction of a second before she jumped. She might have broken her leg had she jumped since it was a pretty high window, but she figured she could at least have hobbled away.

After that, she made another attempt to get away when the UPS delivery man came. Above the bed she slept on was a large, long window that was covered with a curtain. Outside the window were the stairs going up to the front door of the house. At one point, my sister got it that someone was outside on the stairs. Catching everyone in the room off guard, she suddenly jumped up in the bed and, throwing

---

[1] *Although the popular media continue to perpetuate the brainwashing myth, it runs contrary to the standard scholarly position. See appendix for more information.*

the curtain open, she began violently beating on the window and frantically screaming, "Help me, help me!" with all of her strength. In a moment, several people were on top of her, pulling her down and covering her mouth. The delivery man was totally shaken up by the time the wife of the owner of the house came to the door a minute later. He told her, "Ma'am, I think there is a woman inside that really needs help." He said he felt he should call the police.

She just calmly smiled and reassured him that it was only her wild teenage daughters who were just fooling around, having a good time. She said something to the effect that they loved to play jokes and she was going to talk to them. After about five minutes of talking she managed to calm him down, but she could tell as he walked away that he was still a little uneasy. My sister said later that she was just hoping that man would call the police, but unfortunately he never did.

Somehow the room or situation I was in didn't even give me the hope of escape. The room seemed to be always dark, even in the day. At night three or four people were sleeping in the room with me. My brother slept right in front of my bed and there were two or three others in strategic places throughout the room. It was the same with my sister, of course. The only hope of rescue I had was that some of my big strong brothers from the Community would miraculously find us and burst through the door at any moment and save us. My sister told me after the deprogramming that that's what she had hoped for also.

So here they were, using mind control and force to "save" me from the alleged mind control and force which I had never experienced in the Community. Ironically, I was now being subjected to the constant hammering of the accusation that I was forced into the Community against my will. Yet it was only love that had won my heart when I decided to commit my life to the God I had come to know through the Community. I was never once forced in any way to conform to the beliefs of the Community, nor was my will ever violated. I was so attracted to the love the people there had for one another and the love they had for me, and this love is what has continued to keep me. I knew deep in my heart that this love went beyond human love, and that it was the love from God.

SNAPPING

At the beginning of my deprogramming, I thought I would never give in, but as the days went by, they found the inroad, the weak point. It was an area I didn't have much confidence about. That was my upcoming wedding, which should have taken place five days after this kidnapping began. Although I had developed a relationship over the previous two years with the man I was to marry, and although I enjoyed this friendship very much and we got along very well together, I somehow never came to have the same strong feelings for him that he had for me. Sometimes it's just hard to know and judge what your true feelings are, and what your motivation is. I guess I was waiting for some kind of lightning flash in my emotions that would give me confidence as to whether this was the man I was to marry or not. Besides this, I honestly felt very immature and unprepared for marriage. I knew that marriage wasn't just something you lightly step into, and so many people have ruined their lives by making the wrong decision here.

Really, I felt between a rock and hard place. Deep down in my heart I wasn't really convinced that I loved this man like someone you would make the lifelong commitment of marriage with. So on the one hand I was afraid of marrying him, while on the other hand I was afraid of making a mistake by not marrying him. I doubted myself, since this brother had a wonderful reputation, and his sincerity and love for God was indisputable, and so seemed his love for me.

In addition to this, certain people in the Community who I really respected and looked up to for spiritual advice and guidance, and who also had a relationship with the both of us, were favorable towards this marriage. Yet no one had ever said, "You need to marry this man," or, "It's God's will." I wavered a lot during those two years, not really knowing what was in my heart. At one point the whole thing had even been called off.

Spiritual struggles are not uncommon for disciples. It is normal for those who experience salvation to go through things. The many circumstances that we constantly encounter in the Community bring out what's in us. That's why we are here, to see what's motivating us, and to be healed from every impure, selfish motive, meaning what is not from love. That is what salvation is all about. If there weren't any problems, there would be no need for salvation. But somehow I concluded that the problems that I encountered in my life when this relationship was called off were due to the fact that I didn't give myself to it, and that the solution to those other problems was to be found in this marriage.

Convincing myself like that in my own mind closed me off from the objective advice that I could have received from friends in the Community, had I been totally open and honest with them as to where I was really at in this relationship. Years later I learned that this lack of openness and honesty was my downfall. I would have gone into this marriage to get out of some problems, but not because I had a love in my heart for the man I was to marry. Had I been open and honest about my inner struggles, most likely it might have been called off altogether, or I might have been counseled to take more time to find out what was really inside me about it.

But once I had declared that I wanted to marry him, it was of course believed to be my true heart, and since people were favorable towards it and no one objected, the matter was a "done deal." But as always, and so also in my case, the word of God proved to be 100% true and trustworthy. "…But he who doubts is condemned, because in whatever he doubts, that is not from faith; and whatever is done apart from faith is sin" (Romans 14:23). Doubts will come back on us in time of testing. And the reality is that we have nothing firm on which to stand. And doubts did come back on me.

Therefore all the accusations and lies spoken during the deprogramming had little effect on me because I had conviction about these other things, until it came to this one statement: "We know that you don't love this man you were going to marry." That's what got me. At first, I vehemently swore that I loved him and that I was going to marry him when I got out of this mess. But after three days of hearing this over and over, I had begun to entertain the thought. Really, this statement exposed my deepest fears and doubts. Perhaps I didn't have to marry this man after all, something I had only imposed upon myself.

Suddenly, I started laughing and laughing. I remember how worried my brother Eric was. I think he thought that I had really lost my mind. I was laughing because I was relieved when I realized that I actually didn't have to marry him. Unfortunately, it had to be under these circumstances when it became clear to me what was in my heart for this man.

In the hours that followed, I really went through hell in my emotions. Somehow, I was so sad. I loved my friends in the Community so much — surely God was with them! "But why did this happen?!! How did I come to the point that I was about to marry someone I didn't truly love?" I didn't understand at the time that the problem was with *me*. There was so much confusion in me. I couldn't explain anything anymore. Nothing made sense. Of course, the deprogrammers told me that for sure this happened because the Community was a cult.

After this, I seemed to have little resistance against their onslaught of accusations, although I somehow knew that it was all so absurd. They had found the crack, the weak point that burst the dam wide open. This is what they call "snapping." I think my sister "snapped" sometime the next day.

Then Naomi Goss, a woman who had been kidnapped from the Community and deprogrammed a few months before, showed up with Ted Patrick. I really only knew her by name, as she hadn't lived in the Community very long. Now she obviously was on the other side. They wasted no time. They showed us video after video of the testimonies of other people who had been deprogrammed from different so-called "cults" — Divine Light Mission, Sun Myung Moon, Children of God, Hare Krishnas, Scientology — always trying to compare them as much as possible with our community.

Mr. Patrick and Mrs. Goss quickly made a video of my sister and me — our testimony of how we had been deceived into this evil cult. There was so much pressure and it all went so quickly that I hardly understood what was going on. My conscience tearing me up, my mind in total confusion, they rushed us to the radio and TV stations to speak out against the Community. This was where I met Melinda again, as she was the one who escorted us to these places along with Ted Patrick. Really it was a nightmare. They seemed in such a hurry to do this. It all went very fast.

I learned later that they do this because sometimes people start "floating." This is a deprogramming term for a person who starts doubting the deprogrammers and what they are saying and starts missing the "cult" and desiring to return. So they rush you through this process, hoping it will strengthen your mind against the "cult" you had just come out of.

Afterwards I felt so terrible. If God was truly with those people, whom in my heart I still loved so much, then I had become the most treacherous person for speaking out against them. If He wasn't with those people, then for me He absolutely couldn't exist and I didn't believe in God anymore.

After having a chance to reflect a little over the next few days, I couldn't help but notice how Naomi Goss was walking around in tight, flashy clothes and smoking like a chimney. Even though it was the Christmas season, it wasn't a cover-up for her lewd behavior. After I snapped, one of the first things she and Mary Alice Chrnalogar, a young women who was also on the deprogramming team, asked me was, "Do you want to get your hair cut? When are you gonna cut it?" They were so eager for me to cut my hair. It was obvious that I was surrounded by strong, independent women whose life was in their own hands no matter how much they said they trusted in God.

Ted Patrick cursed all the time, especially when my mom wasn't around. When we had gone to the Chattanooga Choo-Choo for the TV interview, I remembered how I had gone with Naomi Goss to Patrick's red velvet suite, which was in an old train car that had been turned into a hotel. There was an unmade double bed with red satin sheets. Actually, the decor of the whole room was entirely red satin, giving it kind of a sleazy atmosphere. I wondered whether he paid for all of that with my dad's money. Just the way Patrick and Goss were with each other made me wonder. Somehow, I felt uneasy about it.

Because of the holidays there was a lot of rich food and a lot of celebrating going on, which I hadn't been used to for a while. The man who owned the house where the "deprogramming" happened was really hard for me to take. He had offered his house for the deprogramming. His daughter, Mary Alice, who really wanted me to cut my hair, had been kidnapped and deprogrammed from a group in northern California, I believe, called *The Lighthouse*, and now they had joined the "cause." He was kind of a brawler and was half drunk most of the time. He was more than merely a social drinker. His big beer belly, crude passes and bad jokes totally repelled me. Actually, the shock of it all was pretty hard to take.

Honestly, I was taken aback when I first met Ted Patrick. I was expecting a somewhat educated-looking person, but instead he appeared to me more like a slick-talking street con, or even less than that — a shady, illiterate bum. The way Patrick and Goss were even seemed to bother my mother. It's amazing what con artists those two were. My mother was probably more bothered about Ted than Naomi. This was the sense that I got. I think my mother really lowered herself to get what she wanted, so I guess the thing that comforted her was that the end would justify the means.

I don't know whether it was part of Ted's planned routine or not, but he brought this whole big rap about it all being a "commie plot." He had a whole theory behind the emergence of cults in the US, which really played on my mom's interest in politics. He claimed it all started in 1917. The communists had proclaimed that they would take over the US without firing a single shot. They'd declared that they would destroy us from within, through the media, the educational system, and the religious system. So he said that the emergence of cults was the breakdown of the religious system, as there were many thousands of young people that are being sucked into these cults every day and all coming under the authority of a few cult leaders. He spoke about a picture of several cult leaders shaking hands with some communist leader. It was one of those pictures that was continually promised but that was never presented. It was so obvious how he played on her fears, telling many horror stories of things that happened to other ex-cult members, his workers backing him up with their own testimonies and always trying to relate it to our community and the "evil" workings behind it. Ted spoke about these things with a lot of passion, bringing up his firsthand experience of his son almost being taken in by one of these cults, and how he just barely made it out of there. He acted like a dramatic con artist, shoveling it to her "big time." I think he really had my mother.

A few days after the interviews we went to Alabama to Naomi Goss' sister's house. She had also been involved in my deprogramming, and she was also pretty devoted to the cause. She was an overweight, strong Christian woman who was totally convinced about the evils of cults and how people need to be delivered from those places. She had short, tight, curly hair and wore a man's baseball shirt, which was at least three sizes too small, over her large upper torso. She was strong and intimidating and far from having a "gentle and quiet spirit," as 1 Peter 3:1-4 describes and as we were taught in the Community.

While we were there, we met two other couples who had been deprogrammed from our community a few months earlier, Larry and Ronda, and another couple, whose names escape me. They were from La Grange, Georgia. I was amazed about how little they actually had to say about the Community in Chattanooga, but what they did say was of course only negative. Even though they declared how glad they were that they had gotten out, there was kind of a sadness about them. One of the couples seemed to be especially quiet. I was surprised to learn that they had just gone through a divorce. This happened after they were taken from the Community a few months before. Nobody seemed to say anything about this! But come on! What happened?! It didn't seem like they were having such a good time since they were rescued from that "evil place."

One of the few things we were supposed to do during our short visit in Alabama was to also speak with a Baptist preacher who actually had some of the Community's teachings and who tried to point out where it was doctrinally off. What he had to say really didn't mean a whole lot to me. It was hard for me to pay attention. As I recall, I felt he was totally lost with those teachings and didn't really know what he was talking about. He rambled through this stuff and never delivered the punch. I kept thinking, "So what is he trying to tell me? That I should live like him?" Actually it just depressed me.

Meeting these people was all part of the agenda that was supposed to strengthen us. Everything was pretty rushed. We were on a tight time schedule.

Last but not least, we were supposed to see a horror film about the Jim Jones tragedy in Guyana. I don't see how this film could fail to put fear into anybody. It affected me a lot, but who knows how much of it was even true? Of course, these Christians use it as absolutely unbiased documentary to support their cult-scare agenda.

THE REHAB IN SAN DIEGO

From there we went straight to a rehabilitation center in San Diego near Ted Patrick's house. I was told that at that time there were two rehabilitation centers in America for people who were coming out of cults: One was in San Diego, California, and one in Iowa City, Iowa. The rehabilitation center was also an essential part of the deprogramming. Ted's daughter Ann was running the place, as it was her condo. Contrary to her father, she was a very sweet and gentle person. She really didn't get into the whole thing and didn't interfere much as far as talking to these ex-cult members who stayed in her house. It seemed that she was pretty much living her life apart from her father's occupation.

Anyway the minimum amount of time a person has to stay is two weeks, and the maximum time is six weeks. I guess it supposedly depends on how a person is doing psychologically, but I think the bottom line is how much money you have. It's incredible how much money is being spent.

Basically, the purpose of the rehab is to get people totally away from the so-called cult they were involved in and to rehabilitate them into society again, with the hope that they will adjust if the deprogramming was successful. They go about this by taking you out to dinner to your favorite restaurants, whether it's Chinese or Mexican food, whatever *you* desire — night clubs, discos, ice cream parlors, flea markets, movie theaters, swimming, or shopping. It's all about *YOU*. You can pretty much do any activity you want, and if you lack initiative or ideas, someone is constantly suggesting some kind of entertainment for you. They only require that you go to Dr. Dean's hypnotic show at some night club, just to show you the real power of hypnosis and what you were under, and suggest that you would see the horror movie about Jim Jones again. I hardly could get much out of Dr. Dean's show. I felt like I was in a typical night club in Vegas watching some magic show.

There was always a bodyguard assigned to you, someone who made a schedule with you, taking one day at a time. This person kept tabs on you as to how you were doing emotionally and psychologically, whether you were *floating* and drifting back to wherever they got you out of, or if you were making the switch and adjusting to "normal" society again. In our case, this person was Naomi Goss. She would accompany us wherever we went. It was so obvious to me that she was personally getting something out of this — walking around in her tight clothes, puffing on her cigarettes as she called the shots. And of course all of this was paid for by my dad. I knew that we were really blowing his money.

Actually, it was all very mind-blowing for me. I couldn't really enjoy it because I knew deep down that something was *really* wrong. In the Community I was learning that true satisfaction and fulfillment comes from denying yourself and living for others, by laying your life down for your brothers and sisters. I had experienced the joy and peace that came from having a good conscience. Now everything was centered around me and my pleasure, with Naomi constantly reassuring me, "It's okay, it's totally normal. That's what love is. Whoever loves you wants you to have a good time and they'll pay for it. You can see that in the Community they didn't really love you because they didn't put the money out for you." It seemed so shallow to me. Looking at Naomi, really all of these people, merely confirmed the fact the more self-centered people are, the more superficial they are.

I remember one night going to a fancy night club. We discussed on the way over that my sister and I were under age to drink alcohol. Naomi said we would just lie about it if we were asked. It'd be okay. For sure we looked 21 anyway. It was things like this that made me feel like the rug just got pulled out from underneath my feet. I didn't understand the morality of it all. Swearing, drinking, smoking, lying, blowing my dad's money, being immodest and seductive — none of these things seemed to bother her or anybody else. It didn't seem there was much of a conscience there, and that's their business, but how could they be delivering me from some "evil" cult? I didn't get the inconsistency. It seemed so ironic. I had always felt that my dad had some common sense. But now it seemed as if my parents had really lost it.

Sometimes I got distracted with having "fun," sometimes I thought it was alright, but most of the time I was miserable inside. I had no peace, was totally anxious and tense, a nervous wreck. I couldn't sort things out, churning them over and over again in my mind. I couldn't figure out what had happened. I gained 30 pounds in three weeks. I felt bad that my parents had to spend so much money. Surely the rehab was as expensive as the deprogramming. It was outrageous. My parents must have spent a fortune on the whole thing.

BACK "HOME"

After the two weeks at the rehab my parents, took us to Mexico, from Tijuana on down to Ensenada. A week later, we were back in Oakland, California. My parents were really paranoid. Sometimes they had us get down in the car, thinking someone in the Community was after us. We noticed how one of them would come home from work every day at a certain time, five minutes before the mailman would come, and they would wait for the mail so they could intercept any letters from anyone in the Community. One time we got to the mail before they did and we were able to receive a precious letter from a good friend, which we secretly read several times. It made me miss the relationships I had in the Community so much.

I think my parents were filled with a lot of fear and guilt, which drove them to such extreme measures — fear because of the cult paranoia that especially the deprogrammers and cult awareness groups had put into them. Everything was a "cult" and would end up like Jim Jones if it wasn't Baptist or Lutheran — straight down the middle. And guilt, maybe, because of the lack of time they had spent involved with us as children. I'd say my parents tried, but I think they just didn't understand our real needs and how to meet them. Besides this, they weren't able to compete against the peer pressure. Business and other things were many times more important to them, and suddenly the years were gone, and now they felt so responsible that we had ended up in a "cult." I think deprogrammers really take advantage of parents in this state who are seeking help, telling them that love will pay any price. It's really sad, but that's how they get them to pay such high prices. It's obvious what hucksters they are.

Back in Oakland we began to see Margaret Singer, a well-known psychiatrist in the Bay area whom Ted Patrick had suggested to my parents that we should see. We had one appointment with her, and after that we couldn't get in touch with her anymore. She no longer would answer the door or her phone. We wondered what was going on. It seemed so strange. Then we found out that the Mills family, defectors from *People's Temple* before the Guyana tragedy, whom she had been seeing, had just been murdered. She had been receiving strange threatening phone calls during this time. It seemed too much for her. She was really afraid. There was a lot of publicity about the Mills, and I remember seeing another man on TV from Florida. He was one of the last few defectors from Guyana, and he was saying, "If you find me dead somewhere and it looks like an accident, don't believe it!! They're killing every last one of us. I'll probably be next."

He seemed really terrified. The whole thing was very mysterious and frightening.

The next twenty months were extremely difficult for me. I can pretty much say that I came out of this whole deprogramming convinced that there wasn't a God. I just couldn't believe that He would have allowed me to be deceived by an evil cult after I had cried out to Him with all of my heart two days before I came to the Community, begging Him that if He was real that He would please reveal Himself to me. As far as I was concerned, if the Community was a cult, then God didn't exist, because they were the closest thing I had ever seen to God as far as an expression of His character and what He must be like.

In the deprogramming, they try to combat the beliefs of the Community with Christian doctrines. It must have been my parents' desire that I would become a Christian, but offering me Christianity at this point was like a bad joke. It was like someone offering me a stale, dead, white wafer after eating good whole-wheat bread for four years — experiencing the warmth, love, and care of my brothers and sisters, and then saying to me, "Be warm and well fed, and find a good Bible-believing church somewhere." Ah! It hurt too much to think about... "Good-bye happiness, hello loneliness… I think I'm gonna die…"

I got my driver's license and to somehow survive, threw myself into four part-time waitressing jobs and a full load in college. I tried to go on doing as I saw everybody else doing — just forget pondering about the meaning of life. My father used to say, "If I have to go through life, I'd rather go through it rich. If this is all there is, you might as well be comfortable." So here I was, leveled and reduced to the thinking that I needed a good education so I could get a good paying job, so I'd be happy in life! That's just the way it works in the world.

This attitude left me feeling bitter and getting old real fast. Everyone around me thought I was doing well because I was making good grades and working all the time. I almost had my car paid for and was in the process of getting an apartment, having paid the first and last month's rent. I also put a lot of money and time into the preparations of refurnishing it according to my own liking, since I thought I'd be there a long time. Even though I enjoyed doing these kind of things, and at times was distracted by it, I was always aware of an inner emptiness. Outwardly it looked like I was making it, but inside I was miserable. What was the point in life, all my efforts doing this and that, if I didn't know why I was created? What was the point to it all? These questions once again plagued me. "Hello darkness, my old friend, I've come to talk with you again." This sad melodic tune of emptiness and despair could be heard across the land from bars to cars. Though it was being sung in many different ways and in many different voices, the underlying theme was always the same.

For comfort, I started to drink again, a little here, a little there, afraid to totally let go. I basically lived off cigarettes and coffee, since for a waitress coffee is always free. For the most part, waitresses seem to be pretty unhappy people, surviving on the mentality, "another day, another dollar." I had no desire for relationships. There seemed to be no lasting basis for them after experiencing the deep relationships in the Community. Yet I was lonely.

My sister was doing even worse. She took it pretty hard. Right away, she had gone back to Pat, her old boyfriend, and her old ways. She would go through deep depressions, and was even suicidal at times. I could hardly reach her. And if I did, what could I tell her? "Life's great!" No one knew what we were going through and no one could ever understand the confusion. Somehow, this question about God was never settled for me.

THE TURNING POINT

One day, half drunk, I started talking to my mother. I asked her why she had spent $20,000 putting hardwood oak floors into her house instead of taking in the homeless poor and reaching out to needy people, such as I was when I came to the Community. Isn't that what Jesus wanted — that we would help people and offer them our life and our home, everything we had, as we did in the Community? She got pretty flustered and riled up. Looking me straight in my face, she said, "Why don't you just go back there then!"

Actually, I think she was just trying to play some reverse psychology on me, trying to deal with my ungratefulness, but I'll always be thankful for the effect her question had on me. It stunned me, even in my intoxicated state, and caused me to really question myself as to why I didn't just go back. In this moment, I realized that it wasn't fear or confusion that was holding me back anymore, but that even though I hated my life and the mess I was in, I still loved the comforts of it, and this I told her. It was one of those moments in life when everything is crystal clear. This was a real turning point for me.

One night, when I was working at a banquet hall in Jack London Square, I decided to do it! I couldn't hold back what was in my heart anymore. After work I went to the old phone booth. My hands shaking, I pulled the phone number out of my pocket and began putting the change in from my tip money. "I wonder if they'd be really strange by now, maybe wearing all black or something." I was nervous, thinking that maybe they couldn't forgive me for speaking against them and I would be rejected. That's what the deprogrammers said about one man who tried to go back to the place from which he was deprogrammed, implying that this would probably happen to me, too, if I decided to go back.

Suddenly, I heard a voice on the other end. To my surprise, I was warmly greeted with excitement. I was so relieved. After talking for a few minutes, I asked, "What are you guys doing now?" I'll never forget the answer: "Well, we are still learning to love one another." I thought it was the most wonderful thing I'd ever heard. Is there anything better that you could do with your life? I was getting ready to throw in my chips. I would rather be wrong with these people than right with my miserable life out here.

Shortly after this, I remember breaking down inside on my way to work. I decided to make myself vulnerable and to trust just one more time. Once again, I prayed with all my heart, "God, if You are real, please, please reveal Yourself to me. Where are You and who are You with?" Could He hear me? Did He ever hear me? Could He see me? Did He care? The answer came just a few days later.

THE RETURN

It was a warm summer night in the end of August 1981. I was with my sister on the front porch of our parents' house, drinking vodka and smoking cigarettes, when I noticed a man slowly walking up the street past our house. At one point, he stopped and looked as though he was straining to recognize us. It was dark out and I couldn't see who it was, only his silhouette. After a moment, he continued until he was out of sight behind some trees. It was one of those rare times my sister and I spent together sharing our hearts with one another. I continued having a good time with her.

Suddenly, I heard someone coughing from behind the trees. Was that man still out there? Did he not continue walking? It made me a little uncomfortable and I asked my sister if she wanted to go inside. I thought maybe it was one of her crazy boyfriends. We went to her bedroom, whose windows faced the road. After sitting there listening to Neil Young for a while, I suddenly heard a loud, piercing whistle. She leaned backwards out the window and laughed, yelling, "What do you want?!"

I heard a familiar voice that seemed to be coming back through years of time. "It's me, Gene. If you want to see Marsha or me, we're down at my sister's house."

It was as if time stood still. My sister yelled back, "Okay." I knew that the moment of decision had finally come for me. I couldn't run away anymore. I probably would have sat there indefinitely if it weren't for my sister who kept telling me, "Come on, let's go see'um. Come on, get ready. Fix yourself up," leaning toward the mirror as she redid her bright red lipstick.

After two hours of procrastinating, I found myself walking down the street. Hope and fear filled my heart at the same time. Could I be forgiven for what I had done? Was there hope for me? And if there was, was I willing to completely give my life, to surrender? Smoking my last cigarette on my way down, I gathered together enough courage to go and knock on the door. After a few moments of suspense, they were right in front of me — a moment I had often imagined, wondering what it would be like. I suddenly felt so dirty and ashamed, and at least ten years older. Their smiling faces only showed forth warmth and acceptance. They were so happy to see us. They invited us in, and as we sat down in the living room, Gene's nephew pulled up a chair as well. He probably had heard a lot about his uncle, and out of curiosity he wanted to get in on this one.

Gene told us that this was the second time he had come out to California to see us and wondered whether we had ever gotten his message to meet him at Half Moon Bay in Monterey a year before. He told us his sister was supposed to give us the message. For some reason she never did. Hindered to speak too much at this point, he simply asked my sister whether she wanted to see him again. Indifferently, she replied, "No, not really." Then he asked me if I wanted to see him again. I said, "Yes." So we made an appointment to see each other the following day.

We planned to meet after I finished my lunch shift at the Kaiser building in a park across the street. I was so excited, I could hardly endure as I kept watching the clock. For from the moment we first talked together, my heart began to respond. It wasn't just their words. It was a new song — different from the world. It was the song of the Community. I had heard it before and almost forgotten. It was a song of hope and love, a song of faith and forgiveness.

The next day as we talked, he asked me if I wanted to go to Germany. There was a small community there, and he was thinking maybe I would want to go there to avoid further trouble with my parents. I agreed to go. It took me about a week to get my passport together. I met them on Monday, and by late Friday afternoon I was on an airplane to London — but not without an intense and highly emotional family encounter right at the end before I left.

That Friday morning I woke up very early to finish packing my things. I then wrote a note to my parents, so they wouldn't think I had been murdered or something. I stuffed the note in the side of a brown paper bag that had some of my things in it. My mother was also up very early — 5 o'clock, as usual — to pray and study, since she was a teacher of Bible teachers. I had been telling my parents for a few days that I was moving into my apartment on Friday, so it wouldn't seem strange to them. I then took a shower, but when I got out I sensed there was something wrong. For one thing, my dad was awake and nervously walking around, and what's more, my brother was also. They both never got up before 8 a.m., and by that time I was always long gone.

With red eyes my father kept asking me, "Honey, where are you going?" I told him I was moving into my apartment today. A few minutes later he would oddly ask the question again. Getting slowly frustrated, I would always give him the same answer. When it was time to go I said goodbye, and relieved, went up to my car. They all stood on the porch looking at me as I tried to start my car. I turned the key but nothing happened. My heart sank. My car always starts. Now it wasn't even making a noise. I tried many times but it wouldn't start. It was obvious to me that they had done something.

I opened the door and yelled at them, "Fix my car!" They just stared at me with sad blank faces. Familiar fears came back. I was almost hysterical. I didn't know what they were up to. Were the police on the way? Did they make arrangements to put me into some kind of institution, since the deprogramming didn't work? Should I just try to make a run for it and get away with my life? I continued to yell at my brother to fix my car until my parents told me to calm down and come inside so we could talk. I didn't know whether I should trust them or not. Finally I went inside with them.

My mother told me how she was going through my things while I was taking a shower and found the note. My mother was so intuitive. I remember how she could even smell a match burning clear over on the other end of the house. My brother said I was just "floating" and that I didn't really want to go back there. He said he'd give me six months and I'd be back again. I reminded them that they promised me if I wanted to go back to the Community when the deprogramming was over, I could. It had been almost two years now and I told them that I was sure that I wanted to go back. Anxiously I demanded that my dad would tell my brother Peter to fix my car. He then told him to do it as he had pulled some wires. I think they let me go without putting up further resistance because they probably felt obliged to keep their promise. Their later actions seemed to prove that they bitterly regretted their decision.

I had half a day left to tie up some things before leaving. In the end, I miraculously made it to the San Francisco airport by 5 o'clock. It was amazing how the way just opened up. We made it through rush-hour traffic on the Golden Gate Bridge in record time. I know angels had something to do with this, even how I made it on with a standby ticket. We came in the last minute up to the gate, which was full of people who wanted to get on. They took only the first ten people on the waiting list, and I was number 29, but somehow I ended up on the flight.

Kirsten Nielsen(left) with her husband Martin Mueller
in the Community in Sus, France, 1984

FRANCE

It was now August 1984 — three years after I had returned. In the meantime, I had come to know and fallen in love with a German brother. As it was, we had gotten married the previous April. After traveling for one year in southwestern Europe, looking for a new home, the small but growing community in Germany settled into an old château in southern France. It was nestled in the quaint village of Sus, in the lowlands of the Pyrenees Mountains. On certain days you could see the awesome view of these majestic snow-capped mountains. We named it *Tabitha's Place* in honor of a young French woman, the first disciple from France, who had come to live with us while in Germany. It was the end of a beautiful summer.

Kirsten Nielsen(left) with friend Charlotte Stringer (right)
in the Community in Sus, France, 1984

THE SECOND KIDNAPPING

My husband Martin and I and some others had just returned from a trip to Holland, where we had picked up some good friends at the harbor in Amsterdam. When we got home to Tabitha's Place, people told me right away that my sister was staying in a hotel in Navarrenx, the neighboring town, and had been urgently trying to get in touch with me for several days. Her visit was very unexpected. Not having seen her in about three years, I was quite surprised about this visit, especially that she'd come all the way to France. It made me feel a little uneasy since my relationship with my parents hadn't improved too much. They had never expressed that they were sorry for kidnapping me, and so it made it hard for me to trust them. As far as I knew, my sister was still living with them.

I had to remember a promise that she and I had made together after our deprogramming, that if either of us ever wanted to go back to the Community, we wouldn't tell on each other, and we would never hinder each other from doing what was in our heart. It was a very serious and solemn promise we made, no light thing, as no one else could ever begin to understand what we had been through.

She said she was just traveling through Europe, and since she was in France, she really wanted to come and see me. She was pretty down and out. It all sounded really convincing, but the last thing she said was, "Whatever happens, just remember that I love you." This should have warned me, but I didn't want to catch on because of what I was going through at the time, and her company was comforting.

Somehow these situations always seemed to come upon me whenever I was going through some deep things. Although I madly loved my husband, we were going through some struggles adjusting to each other, as we had gotten married in a flash. I don't want to call it 'world at war,' but if I say that I came from a big city in California and he from a small town in western Germany, you may understand what I'm talking about.

Anyway, as a precaution, two of my friends from the Community who had known my sister from before went to the hotel to meet with her first. While they were there, they pretty much concluded that something strange was going on. When they talked to her they felt she was nervous and uneasy. They asked the woman at the desk whether my sister had come alone or with someone else. She said, "Yes, she is with those two men over there," pointing to two men who were sitting at a small table together. As my friends passed by the table of these two men, they noticed a Hertz rental car key lying on the table. They were speaking Italian. This for sure didn't line up with her story that she was down and out and traveling alone through Europe.

She was so nervous that at one point she abruptly got up and disappeared down the hall and into another hotel room, which also seemed strange to them. When they came back from seeing her, they warned me that she probably was not on the up-and-up about things. She still wanted me to come alone to the hotel and see her, but we arranged that I would meet with her in an outdoor restaurant in Navarrenx with three of my friends. When we met, she had a strange story and no one really believed it.

Over the next three days, she came to our place and spent time with Martin and me. I think Martin liked meeting my sister, but he couldn't quite understand all this kidnapping stuff, as he hadn't grown up on American thrillers. He couldn't believe that anyone in their right mind would conceive of such a thing. Anyway, I had been advised not to go out of the gates alone with my sister because we didn't know whether we could trust her motives, so we did laundry together and the three of us talked and took walks together. I found out later that many times over those three days people were hiding in the trees and in the bushes, behind dirt mounds, in corn fields, and behind old stone walls, with rope and tape, just waiting for us to get close enough so that they could jump out and grab Martin, tie him up, gag him, and leave him down by the river or wherever, and make off with me.

Martin, totally oblivious to everything, kept ruining their plans, because whenever we would start to get close enough for them to jump out and grab him, he would change his mind, choosing another direction or a different time to go to a specific place my sister would suggest. And though she would persist, he wouldn't go. This frustrated the kidnappers, who had to be careful that no one saw them in the vicinity. One time they had to stay out a whole long summer day in a sweltering corn field with their walkie-talkies, swatting flies.

On the morning of the third or fourth day, I got offended at my husband about something. In the rush of emotion, I didn't care about the advice I had been given concerning my sister. Being in denial about her possible ill motives, I took off with her *alone* down to the river. Near the river we stopped and talked, sitting down on some big stones under the shade of some trees. It was peaceful and I had calmed down. Suddenly I heard the sound of walkie-talkies. Despite the uneasiness of others in the Community, I had been convinced that she was not up to anything. So the sound did not alarm or frighten me even when three men came around the corner from behind some trees and headed across the field toward us, one having a rope in his hands. Not recognizing them at all, I just thought they were fishermen, as there were often lots of them in the area. Besides that, my sister very calmly made a silly gesture and laughing, she said, "We're coming out with our hands up." It was so silly, but I couldn't help but laugh.

Stopping one foot away from me, I was totally shocked when I suddenly recognized two of them as my brothers. Everyone was still for an instant. No one knew what to expect. Thoughts raced through my mind. I remember in the last deprogramming how my resistance made them react so much more, making it much harder for me. I guess they had been in these cornfields for a while, and it seemed they were itching for action. I decided to play along with it until I had a chance to easily get away. I thought going along with it would make it easier on me, as I felt I didn't have it spiritually or emotionally to resist them, not realizing that this decision would cause me agony in my conscience even years afterwards. I suddenly broke into a smile and said, "It's funny, this is the only way we ever meet. I'm glad you're here. You're right on time. I wanted to leave anyway." It caught them a little off guard. They looked at one another, not knowing what to really think or what to do. Then they grabbed me, and my brother said, "Come on, hurry! Let's get her to the car!"

Holding onto me, my two brothers ran with me around the bend towards the river, then cut through the edge of a cornfield and across to another dirt road where a white car was waiting for us. They flung open the back door and threw me in, holding my body down. As they did this, I realized that my mother was sitting in the front seat. They raced down the road to the main road, following close behind another car, and together they sped away from Tabitha's Place.

In the long ten-hour ride to Paris, my kidnappers were quite tense and afraid. They kept close watch on me at all stops, always sending two or three with me to the restroom. We hardly ever stopped at a rest stop, but always in the fields. I remember them anxiously discussing the fact that I didn't have a passport and what they could do about this matter. I didn't do much talking in the car, but when I did, I lied and said things that would make them believe I wanted to leave anyway. They seemed quiet and perplexed.

THE SECOND
DEPROGRAMMING

When we got to Paris, we went straight to an old apartment building, to a room that was on the second floor. It was an old man's small private apartment. I found out that he had a daughter who was deprogrammed from some other group in America, and out of sheer gratitude that she had been set free, he lent out his apartment for this kind of business. All the doors had double locks on them.

This time it was another well-known deprogrammer, Joe Alexander, an Italian, who was doing the deprogramming, along with his colleague, a younger man named Charlie. These were the two men who had been sitting at the table in the hotel in Navarrenx, where my sister had been staying. Mary Alice was also with them, the young woman who was on my first deprogramming in 1979. Since then, she had been involved in many deprogrammings, "helping" other people to get out of different groups across the world. At first she had been working for Ted Patrick, but now she was with Joe Alexander. I wondered if she switched because Patrick was facing charges for kidnapping at the time, and his sons for raping a girl during a deprogramming session. Mary Alice's parents had become such "dear" friends of my parents after I had undergone my first deprogramming in their house in Chattanooga, Tennessee,.

This deprogramming, unlike the first one, was more relaxed, probably a lot due to my lack of resistance. I remember sitting in a room with Joe and Charlie, who were talking to me in what seemed a very unprofessional way. Their accusations seemed on the edge of ridiculousness and plain stupid. The only thing they had going for them were the locks on the door.

The springboard for their first accusation was an article from one of our freepapers. I happened to have read this article and it was obvious to me that they must not have read it themselves. Besides that, Joe kept falling asleep while they were talking. Charlie had to keep tapping him with his foot to wake him up. This happened many times over the next few hours. It was obvious that they weren't very well prepared in knowing about the Community, or even in knowing the Bible. It was pretty pathetic. They tried to set up their videotape player, but fortunately it was broken, and so I didn't have to listen to all that. I don't remember very much about this deprogramming. I just remember trying to get it over with, saying as little as possible against the Community, but speaking what I had to in order to convince them.

One evening, my mother brought up the subject about me being married, and she asked whether I was pregnant. I told her that I was. Then she asked, "Are you going to keep the baby?"

Her question stunned me. "Of course I am," I said.

"Well, don't be so hasty," was her reply. "Maybe you should first talk to some of the women at the rehab about it before you make a decision."

My heart felt like it would explode. "Abort my baby?!" I kept thinking. I wondered how far my mother would go with that. Was this comment just off the top of her head, or did she have an agenda? Surely she wouldn't try to put something in my food that would cause me to lose my baby. My mind and my emotions were kind of running wild, but honestly I didn't know what she was capable of. I think my mother was depressed to find out that I was married and pregnant. It all got a lot more complicated then, and she was groping to know how to deal with it. I think they believed that I loved my husband, and Mary Alice so kindly told me that she would even do a deprogramming on Martin for free if he'd ever show up in California. We just would have to provide the plane ticket for her.

Other than her boasting how she had just finished a deprogramming in Israel, I don't remember her being very involved in this deprogramming, except to go on shopping sprees and to buy souvenirs in Paris. I also remember Joe coming into the living room in the evening and saying to my mom, "Hey Joyce, you got some more money for me?" Once again, I couldn't help but feel bad about how she was being taken advantage of by these obvious crooks.

This time my dad didn't come. I only talked to him on the phone. He said he would see me when I got home. He had stayed in California, probably hoping so badly that the deprogramming would work. My brothers seemed a little bored and just hung out.

After about four or five days of this, we went to get passport photos. It was either the same day or the next day that my mother went with me to the embassy. They decided that I would say that I lost my passport while traveling. They seemed nervous. I feel stupid to think about it now, but later I realized that this had been my biggest chance for escape. All I would have had to do was tell the people at the embassy that I was being kidnapped and held against my will and the whole thing would have come to a screeching halt.

There was no problem with getting a passport, and so everyone was getting ready to fly back to the US. It must have been an expensive time to travel as school had just begun, posing another big expense on my mom. I assume that most had round-trip tickets, except myself and Mary Alice, who had just flown in from Israel on a ticket my mom provided for her, and now needed another flight to the rehab in Iowa City with me, as she was assigned to accompany me during my rehab time.

THE REHAB IN
IOWA CITY

The rehab in Iowa City was a lot more low-key than the one in San Diego. Iowa City is a Midwest university town and San Diego is a big city with lots of attractions and high life. The thing that affected me the most were talks there with a couple of women about abortions. One of them gave me her first-hand experience on it. She told me that she was so emotional during her pregnancy, she couldn't stand it, and neither could her boyfriend because she was crying all the time. So when she was four months pregnant she got an abortion and she, as well as her boyfriend, were so glad that she did. I could hardly believe what she was saying. I don't want to say that they counseled me to have an abortion, but for sure no one encouraged me to keep the baby.

The first or second day we were there, Mary Alice got a phone call that her father just had a heart attack and was dying. She was very shocked and sad about this and wanted to go back home to Chattanooga. I comforted her and told her that it would be alright to leave me; I was doing okay. I knew this was my chance. Everything was working out perfectly. Before I got there, the leader of the rehab and his wife had just gone on vacation to visit relatives in Philadelphia. Another worker was gone too. They wanted to assign this one young man to be my "watchdog," so to speak, to go with me wherever I went. I quickly made up an excuse and told the woman who was talking to me about this that I really had a problem with men.

She asked me very sympathetically, "When did you start feeling this way?"

I said, "It all started in high school."

She seemed to really understand, but this created a somewhat difficult circumstance for them, as there was no one else who could be with me. She thought it'd probably be okay if I'd go places alone. After that, I was allowed quite a bit of freedom. I only had to attend a few seminars on psychology and mind control.

GOING HOME

On my third day of being there, I got to go into the city by myself. I went to the university, which was within walking distance, and took a look around. I found a little restaurant on a side street and used the pay phone. I had no phone numbers of any of the communities in America, but at least I could remember the number of Tabitha's Place in France. They had given me $200 spending money from my father, and so I had plenty of change.

Gene happened to be the one who answered the phone. I was *so* happy when I heard his voice, just to have made that contact with my friends again after everything that happened. I quickly told him where I was and what had happened and then we made arrangements on how I could get away. I was to connect with Dicky Cantrell, a friend from one of our communities in America. Everyone called him Gladheart. We were to meet the next day at the public library at 10 o'clock. I was very excited and could hardly wait.

The next morning I packed everything I wanted to take with me in two backpacks. I wrote a note to my father, which I put into the top drawer of the dresser in the room I was staying in. While I was eating breakfast, I talked to the woman who was substituting for the couple who normally was in charge of this rehabilitation center. She was an older woman who seemed nervous and overwhelmed with the responsibility of the job. I tried to put her at ease. I told her that I would really like to go shopping that day, and that I wanted to leave sometime after breakfast. She didn't seem to like the idea too much, although she didn't object, but she told me that I needed to be at a seminar at 1 o'clock. I said, "Okay," knowing that this would make things a little tight.

I went upstairs and got one of the backpacks and came quietly downstairs. I looked at the lady who was in her office. Her back was turned towards me. She was busily working and seemed unaware of me. I quietly went through the kitchen and through the living room. Usually there were at least two or three people hanging around, but amazingly enough no one was there. Then I was out the door, down the stairs, and up the street. At the end of the block, I threw my backpack under some trees. Totally relieved, I ran back to the house. No one noticed that I had been gone. I grabbed my last backpack. Sneaking by her one more time unnoticed, I made it outside again. Throwing the backpack with the other one, I ran back to the house. No one got it.

After I got the last things together, I went into her office and told her that I was going shopping now, and that I'd be back by 1 o'clock for the seminar. Hesitantly she let me go. She didn't like the idea of me going alone. I was really glad that everything seemed to be working out.

I went straight to the public library and waited there by the front door until 10 a.m. Since Iowa City is a university town, there were young people everywhere milling around little shops by the campus. As the minutes drew close, I got more excited, thinking it would soon be all over. 10 o'clock came and went. 10:15... 10:20... 10:30. No Gladheart. My heart began to sink. Then the thought came to me that maybe there was another public library and I was at the wrong one. I went inside the library and asked the woman at the desk if there was another library in town. She said that there was the university library. I got directions and thanked her.

I ran as fast as I could the six blocks, dodging people all the way there. Breathlessly, I looked around. It seemed pretty empty. I was looking for Gladheart's telltale big beard. I didn't see him anywhere. I waited nervously for a few minutes. Then I realized that maybe he had come in this time and was now waiting at the public library. "Oh no, I don't want him to leave," I thought, and started running back to the public library. I arrived totally out of breath and quickly looked around for him. It was getting late. I went into the library and asked the head librarian if a man with a big beard had come in, asking for a blond girl like me.

She answered, "No," so I went out and waited probably 10 or 15 minutes more. Maybe he's come now and is waiting for me at the university library. I decided to check again. I raced back to the university library. I anxiously looked around. He was not there. Time was running out.

"Did you see a man with a big beard who is looking for a girl with blond hair?"

"No."

The young woman at the desk seemed extremely kind and willing to help, so I asked where she would go if she were told to meet somebody at the public library. Would she wait at the public library in the middle of town, or would she wait at the university library? After a thoughtful moment, she asked if I was a university student. "No." Then she asked if the person I was looking for was a university student. "No." "Then I would wait at the public library, if I were you." It seemed like such simple wisdom and it brought me peace.

I took off running as fast as I could through the crowd one more time. As soon as I got back to the public library, I looked around for Gladheart. He wasn't there. I went inside and checked again with the librarian. Irritated, she answered, "No, I haven't."

I decided to wait at the front door until 1 o'clock. That was all I could do. My anxiety was turning to fear, as it was almost 12 o'clock. It seemed it wasn't working out like I thought it would. Suddenly I heard a familiar voice. Without a doubt, it was Gladheart! His first words were, "Turn around slowly," his voice very controlled. He quickly went on to say, "Stay calm, don't act as if you know me, and stay ten paces behind." I wanted to scream and jump up and down and throw my arms around him, but I controlled myself.

As I turned around, I was totally shocked. He had no beard! He had shaved it completely off. Only his mustache was left. He had a nice light blue, button-up shirt on and was wearing round wire-rimmed glasses, and carried a leather briefcase in his hand. He looked like a spiffy, alternative university professor. He casually turned around and walked off. I looked down as it was hard for me to keep from smiling. Nonchalantly, I followed him, looking in shop windows as I walked behind him for several blocks down the cobblestone pedestrian zone until he turned down a side street.

Finally feeling out of danger, we began to talk. "Gladheart! I'm so happy to see you. I've been waiting for you since 10 o'clock."

"Hurry, get in the car! We've got to get out of here! How much time do we have until they notice that you are gone?"

I said, "Until 1 o'clock. They are expecting me for a seminar." Now it was 12 o'clock, so it only gave us one hour.

I think he was handling it pretty well until I told him that we had to get my bags, which I had left under some trees one block from the rehab house. For almost one hour we looked for them, as I had lost my way. All the streets looked the same. I really wanted to get my bags, but besides that, I had also put my passport in one of them. Finally we found the right place. I grabbed my bags and we took off.

Gladheart didn't waste any time, but drove straight to Chicago. Being with him was comforting. I was thankful for his love and concern for me. He had a way of making the worst situations not seem so bad. As we drove, he told me the story of how he had gotten the message to get me, and everything that happened on his end. Believe me, it was quite the adventure — a typical Gladheart story.

From Chicago, we took a plane to Boston, where we spent the night at the Community there. The next day, we traveled up north to the Community in Island Pond, Vermont, where I had lived before, to see my old friends whom I hadn't seen since 1979. I was so happy to see them, and was also very thankful for the people there who paid for my plane ticket. They had been saving the money so that they could fix up their house, but they had given it up for me. I knew that they definitely gave from their substance. These are the kind of people I live with. A few days later, I flew out of New York to San Sebastian in Spain, where I was met by my husband and friends, who brought me back to Tabitha's Place. I was so relieved that it was all over. I was home again.

THE AFTERMATH

I'm writing this 14 years after my last deprogramming. Often I look at my oldest son and I am so glad that he came to birth and that we have him. After my second deprogramming, I told my parents that I couldn't trust them, and that to avoid further harm to myself and my family, I would have to cut off any relationship with them until they gave me clear assurance that they were really sorry for what they had done to me. Unfortunately, up to this day, they never did apologize.

About seven years ago, I had a dream about my dad dying and him calling for me. This really affected me, and I felt I couldn't ignore it. I found out later that he had almost died, but came back to life. Anyway, this caused me to open up communications with my parents again, hoping for a change of heart on their side, and also that they could see us for who we really are. In reality, it was not that we cut ourselves off from them, but they cut themselves off from us through their behavior. There just has to be a certain amount of trust that comes from respecting basic rules of conduct in order to have normal relationships.

Of course, when I became a disciple of the Son of God, I had come out from underneath the authority of my parents, but that doesn't mean that I couldn't have a relationship with them anymore. As a matter of fact, many of my friends in the Community enjoy good relationships with their families. However, my parents never could reconcile themselves to the fact that I had found the Pearl that I had sought for so earnestly, even though my dad always used to tell me growing up, "Honey, the world is your oyster." I guess they didn't like my Pearl and they didn't think it was worth the price I paid for it.*

I'm sure my sister's input about her firsthand experience with the Community didn't help them either. I don't know what prompted them to do the second deprogramming. I could only speculate. I know that my sister changed camps after I came back to the Community. She blamed the Community for many things, although she probably wouldn't even be alive had she not come to the Community when she did — the way her life was going back then. In every encounter that I had with her since the second deprogramming, either in person or on the phone, she expressed a lot of bitterness about her time in the Community. I think in her heart she knows the truth, but she is not willing to listen to it. It seems to me that this is really what is behind her frantic attempts to justify her life and to find fault with the Community.

---

* "Again, the kingdom of heaven is like a merchant seeking fine pearls, and upon finding one pearl of great value, he went and sold all that he had, and bought it." (Matthew 13:45,46)

The reopening of communications with my parents led to a first visit. By that time, I had moved back to America and lived in Vermont. I found out that my brother Peter had gotten married and moved to upstate New York, where his wife was from. This was not so far from where I was living, so we arranged for a visit in his house. My parents flew out from California for this. Even though Peter told me at the time that he was sorry for the kidnapping and deprogramming, and said that he never would do such a thing again, it is clear that he doesn't really see anything good about how I live my life. If it were up to him, he still would want me to leave the Community.

My other brother, Eric, wasn't in on this particular visit. We saw each other at a later time. This has been the only time we've met since my second deprogramming, and nothing really came out of it as far as amends in our relationship.

On that initial visit in my brother's house, my parents expressed that sometimes people who have been in these cults get burned out after being there for 10 or 15 years. They might have had the hope that this could be happening with me and my husband, and that we were possibly looking for a way out. In this, of course, we had to disappoint them.

I think we were just checking each other out on that visit with my family, trying to figure out where everybody is coming from. It is clear that my family never gave up this thing about brainwashing. The sad result of this is that we can't really communicate with each other on a normal level because they automatically label everything we say as the result of being brainwashed. Even though there have been subsequent visits after this initial one, no progress in mending our relationship has been made. They never acknowledged that I had a free will to seek for God the way my heart and my conscience directed me, and they never respected or accepted the choice I made. Not liking my choice made them very susceptible towards the cult scare, causing them to take in the explanation that after all it wasn't really my choice but it was something I did under the influence of mind control. I think this is really the bottom line.

Looking back, my husband and I see that we lacked wisdom in the way we tried to reach out to them. We could have made it easier on them, yet it is also really clear that unless they give up this thing about us being under mind control or being brainwashed, there can be no real healing or restoration between us. It is sad to say, but so far only suspicion, fear, and mistrust have prevailed.

CONCLUSION

To me what is so scary about this cult scare is that once you have labeled someone as a cult, this brands them in such a negative way that anything they say or do is filtered through that prejudiced conception. Even in the name of God, the masses are eventually liable to do anything with the end justifying the means — as history, especially European history, has proven over and over again, the best examples probably being the Spanish inquisition and the holocaust.* The mindset about the Jews even caused them to be seen as less than human and that justified people to treat them accordingly. If a fly is bothering you, you don't have a problem killing it.

The word of God promises that there will be a demonstration of His love on the earth through a people, an expression of love and unity, not forced unity such as communism, but true unity coming forth from the love of God. What's so frightening is that you can't even live together and love other human beings and practice hospitality according to

---

* "They will put you out of the synagogue; in fact, a time is coming when anyone who kills you will think he is offering a service to God." (John 16:2)

the love that's been poured out into your heart by your Creator, without the cult scare specter casting its shadow and the red flags going up, being accused of "love bombing." People are so paranoid of loving or being loved for wrong motives so no one loves anyone anymore or shows kindness and hospitality, because they are afraid of being accused of being a "cult." And even though there might be groups that are taking advantage of the weak for their own gain, yet taking away the freedom of religion which comes in the wake of the cult scare isn't the answer to this problem. People have a free choice, a free will and this must be respected for God has given man the inalienable right to grope for Him according to the dictates of his own conscience. To take this away from a person is truly the greater injustice and crime against mankind.

TEN YEARS LATER:

1994

*After twenty years in the Community, Kirsten wrote this letter
to her parents, in hopes of sharing the reasons why she returned
to the Community and why she chose to live the way she did.*

Dear Dad,

I'm so thankful I'm in a place where I can
experience true life and be near to my Creator. I'm
thankful I was born in such a significant time when
He could be found. A few days ago I got up early and
took a walk. Everything was very dark, but then I
saw it — the morning star. Oh, it was so beautiful!
As I stood there in the quietness, looking at it, I
said to myself, "I know who you are. Yahshua,[1] my
Savior, by You I have been created anew. You are the
Morning Star who dawned in my heart after such a
long and lonely winter night. You are the Lily of the
Valley that blooms after the dark winter that my life
was before I met You. You are the Son of God. I want

---

[1] *Yahshua* is the Hebrew name of the Son of God, commonly
rendered as *Jesus* in the New Testament.

to give You my whole life. You are worth everything. I am totally satisfied with You."

I want our children to have what I have. It's not material possessions or a comfortable life. Though you faithfully provided all those things for me as I grew up, I was not satisfied and had no real life and no real love. Please don't misunderstand me. I'm grateful for everything you did for me and gave me. I believe that you tried to give me the best, according to your ability and understanding. But maybe what I'm writing here can help you to understand why I have chosen a life different from the life you offered me. Even though I didn't go in the way you wanted me to go, I do still love you and care about you.

Words really fail me to express to you how lost and alone I was before I came to the Community. I was without hope and without God in the world. I'm not saying that living in community saves anyone, for surely it doesn't. In fact, without the Holy Spirit man is not meant to live in community. It is a torture chamber for the flesh. A good look around at all the communes and communities that have ended up in immorality and hostility, eventually dividing and falling apart, testifies to this fact. But what I was drawn to in the Community was the life and the love that was there.

This life is like the life that's inside a bud that causes it to open. What's working there is an incomprehensible force. It's like what causes babies to be conceived, what causes them to breathe their first breath, what causes grass to grow, the wind to blow, the clouds to form. It's like what holds the whole universe together, and even causes men to rise from the dead, and if I'm not connected to that force, then I'm dead. That force, that life is Yahshua, the Master of the Universe, and everyone who is not connected to that life source is just a walking dead person, because their spirit has not been made alive to Him. Their spirit is not compatible with God unless they have been reconciled, forgiven, and brought back into fellowship, total unity and oneness with their Creator through Yahshua. He is coming back to marry a bride who is compatible to Him, one who is worthy of Him.

The evil thing about Christianity is that it makes people think they are reconciled to God when they are not. The fruit of Christianity is like the hybrid vegetables you can buy now. They look so big and beautiful, but they have no life in them. The life is in the seed, and because they have no seed they cannot give true life to anyone, since they are dead. You know the old saying, "You can tell a tree by its fruit. A good tree bears good fruit, and a bad tree bears bad fruit." Christianity is a bad tree that bears bad fruit, and though sometimes it looks good, its fruit has no life-producing seed. It's artificial and sterile.

In the Book of Revelation, Yahshua said to the churches that unless they repented of those things He spoke to them about, their lampstand would be removed and He would not walk among them anymore. Obviously they didn't repent, but went into apostasy. The church in Rome developed into the Roman Catholic Church. Just by looking at the Vatican and judging by the Word of God, you can tell that what the true church turned into is completely void of the true life of God, but goes on in its own "glorious" false light. And so on and on, down through the ages, the Catholic Church had many daughters through divisions, factions, and offshoots — the Lutheran Church being one of them. Probably many sincere people tried and still try to make the fruit of that bad tree seem good, but you can't. The only thing God can say now is, "Come out of her, My people."[2]

I'm not saying these things apart from my own experience. When I grew up, church had no life to offer me. And Dad, it shouldn't be hard for you to agree with me on this, should it? I remember you falling asleep almost every Sunday, because you were bored to death. So there was nothing drawing me in church, but when I came to the Community in Chattanooga, for the first time in my life I saw an amazing thing. It's hard for me to explain because it's a spiritual thing, but all I know is that I was drawn. Before I came to the Community, I had come to the place where I doubted that God even existed, or much less, that He loved or cared about me. But through the life and the love that was communicated to me there, I believed for the first time that God not only existed, but that He truly loved me. Deep down I knew that what I was seeing and hearing was the truth. "If any man is willing to do the will of God, he will know whether the teaching is of God..."[3] The life that I saw was fruit that had a seed in it.

---

[2] Revelation 18:4
[3] John 7:17

I don't know what was different about me compared with the other children of our family, but I remember that as a child I had such a longing in my heart to be connected to God. I'm so thankful that He sought after me and found me. "My sheep hear My voice, I know them, and they follow Me."[4] That's the only thing I could write to you when I left to come back here. When His love and His glory were revealed to me through His people, my response was to give my life to Him and to those people who bore His life — to dedicate my whole life to Him and to forsake everything to follow Him wherever He would go. That was my vow, and I'm still determined to keep my vow.

I want to share with you some things I've been learning about the gospel, as it is getting clearer and clearer to us. Whatever is worth having costs you something. It costs giving up something that you love in order to gain something that you love even more. This is what a ransom is[5] — that which is given up to secure what is more valuable. John 3:16 describes the ultimate ransom: God loved the world so much that He gave His only begotten Son as a ransom. This is a comparison. Of course God loved His Son — "His only begotten Son." But the point this verse is trying to make is that God loved the world even more than He loved His only begotten Son. That's why He gave Him up.

In the Old Covenant, a ransom meant "the price of a life," or, "the price paid for what is redeemed." Proverbs 13:8 says, "The ransom of a man's life is his

---

riches." In Matthew 10:37-39 it explains how a man must give his own life as a ransom. He must give what he loves (his own life) in order to gain what is more valuable (eternal life), just as God gave up His own Son, whom He greatly loved, as a ransom in order to gain something that He loved even more. He gave up His one beloved Son so that He could have many beloved sons, as Hebrews 2:10 says. One Son is not enough — He needs many sons.

Why were those who were called or invited in Matthew 22:8 not found worthy? If one hangs on to his own life, and will not forsake what he must forsake in order to have Messiah, then he is not worthy to have Him or eternal life.[6] Mark 8:37 asks, "What will a man give in exchange for his soul?" What will a man give as a ransom? What is the price? What value does eternal life have to him? It is the same exchange as in Mark 10:17-30 and Matthew 10:34-39 — a man must exchange his old life and all his possessions, including his family, his dream home, occupation, etc. But Mark 10:22 shows that the man did not really value the eternal life that he asked for in verse 17 as much as he valued his own life and possessions.[7] These things were and still are the ransom price.

So when Yahshua asked, "What will a man give in exchange for his soul?" He did not just pose a rhetorical question, even though what He said before, "For what does it profit a man to gain the whole world, and forfeit his soul?" could be thought to allude to that. Christians falsely take that verse to

---

[6] 1 John 5:12; Matthew 16:24-26; Mark 8:34-37
[7] Luke 14:33; Mark 10:28-30

insinuate that there is nothing a person could give in exchange for his soul. Well, that is true in a sense, because the redemption of our soul is costly, so costly that nothing in the world can pay it.[8] That's why it says that we "were ransomed from the futile ways inherited from your forefathers, not with perishable things such as silver or gold, but with the precious blood of Christ, like that of a lamb without blemish or spot."[9] The ransom that Yahshua paid with His blood is priceless. But there is an exchange — a real exchange — that a person must make in order to be worthy to receive the salvation that Yahshua accomplished for him.

I hope you don't mind me laboring this point, as it is an essential part of the gospel. Mark 10:29-30 shows what you must give as a ransom — your house, brothers, sisters, wife, father, mother, children, farms, etc. Is there anything less that you could offer as a ransom? Should you hold on to anything at all, if you trust the One who's saving you? He can't save you if you hang on to all your junk or precious possessions or loved ones who are unwilling to follow after Him with you. You simply can't get into the Kingdom with them, as Yahshua labors the point in Mark 10:23-25.

Giving up everything we have, even our own life in this world, as John 12:25-26 says, is the only way possible to not live for yourself any longer, but for Him who paid the price for your salvation.[10] He paid this great price in order for us to now

[8] Psalm 49:7-8
[9] 1 Peter 1:18-19
[10] 2 Corinthians 5:14-15

participate in the will and purpose of God in the Body of Messiah, which is the Community, as Acts 2:44-45 and 4:32-35 vividly describe, in obedience to the same commandments which must always be included in the true gospel, according to the "great commission" in Matthew 28:18-20. No one can be a disciple any other way. There is no other gospel that calls one out of this abnormal, wicked, and perverse secular society, just as the apostles commanded the 3000 in Acts 2:38-41. Acts 2:40 came before and produced the results of verses 41-45. And if anyone proclaims a different gospel from that of the first apostles, Paul said, "Let him be accursed,"[11] for he is actually Satan's servant.[12]

Today, while the greater King is yet far off,[13] we must ransom our own life, giving up our possessions in obedience to the Master's own words in Luke 14:33 and 12:32-34. This is essential for receiving the good news. So where is your heart? Where is the heart of Christians? Yahshua was emphatic when He said that no one can be My disciple who does not ransom his own life,[14] as Matthew 10:34-39 and Mark 10:17-30 further explain and emphasize.

Therefore one must dispossess himself to be worthy of Messiah, and then the life described in Acts 2:44-45 is not so impossible, which is the only way the church can be. Acts 2:44-45 is the result of proclaiming the complete gospel. Each denomination is the result of whichever gospel created it. In other

---

[11] Galatians 1:6-10
[12] 2 Corinthians 11:4,13-15
[13] Luke 14:31
[14] Luke 14:33,26,27

words, if any denomination is different from how the church was in the beginning, in Acts 2:44-45 and 4:32-37, that is because a different gospel created it — not the gospel that was originally proclaimed by the apostles of Yahshua at Pentecost.

In order to obey the gospel, we must give up our entire lives, including father, mother, sister, brother, etc., as a ransom, just as God gave His own Son as a ransom for us. So again, a ransom is necessary to gain what you want more, just as John 3:16 teaches us what it cost God to have the many sons that He wanted and needed.[15] In Isaiah 62:12, the church is prophetically called "sought out, a city not forsaken." The Hebrew word for "sought out" is derusha, which means "necessary, needed, essential." So much were we needed that it required God to offer His own Son as a ransom.[16]

Our response to this great love can't be any less. It is life for life. According to Romans 6:5, our death in baptism must be just as real as His death on the cross. That means that our old life, with all its dreams, hopes, ambitions, and desires, must come to a real end, including our relationship with our own parents if they attempt to hold us back from following Him. That's what repentance is: to surrender your life, relationships, possessions — everything — to the Son of God. If this does not happen, and if our death[17] is not as real as His death, then it's just a mental concept. And if it's just a mental concept, it's as if His blood that was shed to gain or rescue us didn't really

---

[15] Hebrews 2:10-11
[16] John 3:16
[17] John 12:25-26

mean anything. It's just some myth or fairy tale. But that's not true! His death was very real.

A ransom is usually given because someone's life is in danger. I'm thankful that I was rescued from the "strong man"[18] who was taking me to death, to the sea of fire — this was also very real. Eternal death is a very real thing. Not only was I rescued from eternal death, but I was ransomed and freed from captivity, from the bondage of living for myself.[19] We were redeemed from being the possession of an enemy. Our Master's sacrifice to obtain us freed us from Satan's grasp. Our sacrifice for Him, of our own life, possessions, and family, is our ransom to obtain Him.

So you see, Mom and Dad, it's not that I don't love you, but I have to love Messiah more. I had to give you up in order to obey the gospel. To be worthy of Him you have to give up your father and mother, and whatever is dear to you — even your own life. It actually says in Luke 14:26 that you have to hate your father and your mother. Of course, it's not that "I hate you," as if I have some kind of animosity in my heart towards you, but I had to give you up, as well as my brothers and my sister, so that I could be worthy of Messiah. We have to love Him more than anything else. Mark 10:17-30, Matthew 16:25-26, and Mark 8:35,37 is the overwhelming evidence of what I am saying — the Savior's own words, which is the good news of salvation.

In Matthew 13:44-46, whoever wanted the pearl of great price, or the treasure hidden in the field, had to give up everything for it. The same response

---

[18] Matthew 12:29
[19] 2 Corinthians 5:15-16

is required from us who are worthy of Him. What kind of phony faith could a person claim to have if he would not give up His life for Yahshua?

John 12:26 speaks of serving Him where He is. And where is that? Yahshua dwells in every place where He has caused His name (presence and authority) to dwell. These are the only places where anyone can serve Him and obey the gospel. A place means a community in a township,[20] a place where one terminates his own life in this world to serve the Son of God where He dwells.[21]

If one has received faith, it is proven in His obedience to the gospel, for according to Acts 5:32, John 3:36, and 2 Thessalonians 1:8, the gospel is something to be obeyed. To receive the royal invitation to eternal life in the Son of God, one must capitulate as the "terms of peace" require in Luke 14:26-33. Such capitulation, which is the reality of being baptized into His Body on earth, makes a person worthy of Him and eternal life,[22] being registered in the Lamb's Book of Life and sealed with the Holy Spirit of promise.[23]

He won't have us and we can't have Him unless our faith is as real as His, so we must have the faith to no longer live for ourselves.[24] So to do that there must be a way for us to die to our old life, and this is by the faith of Romans 10:17. Unless we have faith (which the rich man in Mark 10:17-30 did not have), we

---

[20] 1 Peter 2:9-15; 1 Timothy 2:8; 1 Corinthians 1:2,10; Malachi 1:11
[21] 1 Corinthians 12:13; Romans 6:2-5
[22] Acts 13:46
[23] Ephesians 1:13
[24] 2 Corinthians 5:15

cannot truly believe in our hearts in the resurrection as Romans 10:9 requires. It is just as great a miracle to believe in our heart in the resurrection as it was for God to raise Yahshua from the dead, for we, too, are raised by the miracle of His Spirit, by whom we make the good confession.[25]

So it is certain that we ourselves cannot pay the ransom price for our sins. But we must pay with our own "flesh" to be crucified with Messiah. We must be baptized into His death, calling upon His name, the name above all names, confessing His absolute sovereignty[26] over our life. This is the only fitting response to hearing the good news from the sent one in Romans 10:14-17, that is, someone who has the authority to proclaim the good news and to communicate faith because he himself has obeyed the gospel and is living a life of faith.

Even though I quote all these scriptures, and it might be hard for you and somewhat laborious to follow, I hope you won't get lost, but endure until the end of my letter. I want you to know that I put a lot of time and thought into this letter. As you can see, I started in the fall and now it is winter, because I had a great burden that you would understand what I'm doing and why I'm doing it, so that you can see my heart. I'm sure you understand the difficulties of finding time and space as a mother, besides my other responsibilities in the Community. But I did not want to let these things keep me from fulfilling my responsibility towards you, my parents, for I do love and care about you. Anyway, the reason why I

[25] Romans 10:9-10
[26] Romans 10:9,13

am so detailed with the scriptures in this letter is so that you can see that what we are saying is not our own words, but is solidly based on the Bible. What we are saying is actually very simple: You can only receive faith if you meet someone who has faith, and you only can live out your faith in a place where that faith is being lived out.

If God had kept His Son from dying, He could not have provided a ransom for us. If we hang on to our life, or hang on to our ransom, we will lose our life. If we shrink back from our own death in baptism, we will not receive His life.

When a person sinned in the Old Covenant he had to provide an atoning sacrifice, a ransom, to pay the price of his sin. But if he would not provide that ransom, or if his offering was not pure,[27] there could be no forgiveness. Of course, receiving forgiveness was not like a business deal. It was based on faith. It depended upon the mercy of a forgiving God who judged each person according to his heart. He righteously forgave based on the ultimate ransom that He would provide in the future by the death of His own Son. So if a person's heart in the Old Covenant was right, he would provide the best, purest sacrifice he could. This was the expression of his faith and of how much he desired to be forgiven. The whole sacrificial system was instituted by God so that Israel would recognize and understand the sacrifice of His Son.

It is the same with us now in the New Covenant.[28] God has already provided the ransom, but we must

---

[27] Psalm 51:17
[28] John 3:16; 12:25

now give our own life as a ransom in order to be worthy of His ransom. Giving our ransom is the expression of our heart and our faith. We have to give up one for the other — we can't have both. We can't benefit from His ransom while holding onto our ransom at the same time.[29] If we hang onto our life, we will lose it. If we give up our life, we will find it. What if God had hung onto His Son and had not given Him as the price of our redemption?[30] He says, "I made you and I bought you. You are Mine."

So remember, a ransom is that which is given up to secure what is more valuable. John 3:16 says He provided the ransom for the world. So now He will entrust His very own life to those who repent and show it by their actions in response to the gospel, as Acts 2:38-41 explains. The 3000 responded to the "many other words," having received faith to obey the gospel.[31]

Yahshua said, "If anyone desires to save his life, he will lose it. But whoever loses his life for My sake will find it." The word desires means prefers, or chooses, or determines, or wills to actually hold onto and refuse to let go of his life, because he loves his life in this world. But John 12:25 says you have to hate your life in this world. You have to hate your life in this present evil age and not be deceived by the "beauty" of the world — you know, the marvel of the Eiffel Tower, a nice plush home, all the stars on Hollywood Boulevard, and other things like this. You cannot love your life in this world system because 1 John 2:15-17

---

[29] 2 Corinthians 5:15
[30] 1 Corinthians 6:20; 2 Corinthians 5:14-15
[31] Romans 10:16; John 3:36; 2 Corinthians 5:15

makes it clear that "all that is in the world — the lust of the flesh and the lust of the eyes and the boastful pride of life — is not from the Father," and that this "world is passing away."[32]

Mom and Dad, what Yahshua says in Luke 14:26 concerning you is explained very clearly in Matthew 10:37. So I did not want to save my own life, but to give it up, including you, Mom and Dad, as a ransom, for I wanted to be worthy of my Master and Savior Yahshua, and be prepared and ready for Him. This preparation is only possible by working for Him in the Body, helping to prepare it for Him as a Bride by the good works I was saved to accomplish.[33]

When I speak of "giving you up," I mean in the sense that you would have no influence or authority over me anymore. It's just the same as when someone gets married — a man comes out from his father's house and authority to cleave to his wife (or a woman to her husband), to begin a new family together. It's even more so with Messiah that we must come out from our old fatherhood, counting everything as loss to gain Messiah.

That doesn't mean that I cannot have anything to do with you anymore. At one time, our Master's family, including His mother, thought He had gone mad, and they wanted to take Him into custody. You can read about this in Mark 3:20,21,31-35. At that time, He made it very clear to them who His real family was: those who do the will of His Father in heaven. His mind and His heart were set to do

---

[32] James 4:4; Matthew 4:8
[33] Ephesians 2:10; Revelation 19:7-8

the will of His heavenly Father. Everything else was subordinate to that, and nothing could sway Him.

I'm sure this was really hard for His family, and especially for His mother. She had been warned by Simeon when her Son was dedicated as a baby in Luke 2:34-35 that a sword would pierce even her own heart. So when that incident happened, when Yahshua made it clear to His mother and brothers who His real family was, part of that prophecy by Simeon was fulfilled. Of course, that was not the only time that a sword pierced her heart. But she was a humble woman — humble enough to receive the suffering and not resist it. She was pierced rather than offended by the words of her Son, and thus she was honored. And for this reason she was not separated from Him, but could continue in a relationship with Him, as you can see from the Scriptures. When our Master was dying, it was clear what His heart was towards His mother — that He really loved her.[34]

This is our heart also, that we want to love and honor our parents. And what makes them honorable is that they would respect the decision that we've made for our lives. And even though they might not understand us, they are certainly welcome to come and visit and continue in a relationship with us. Even though our relationship with our parents is different after we have given our life to our Master Yahshua, in that we are not under their authority anymore, that doesn't mean that we cannot have a continuing friendship with them. Our decision doesn't have to cut them off from us. Our decision cuts us off from

---

[34] John 19:27

being under their authority, but not from having a relationship with them. They are still our parents, and we appreciate our parents for having raised us. And of course, we understand that they still have an interest in us, which is just normal, but they cannot control and direct our lives anymore. So what cuts off our relationship with our parents is when they don't respect our decision and try to interfere with it. In this case, the word of our Master is fulfilled — that He didn't come to bring peace, but a sword.[35]

Everything will be judged by the word of God, and His word is a double-edged sword, dividing between bone and marrow, revealing the thoughts and the intentions and motives of a person's heart. It's all according to a person's heart as to how he will be judged. The clearest way a person's heart is revealed is by the way he responds to the Word of God, just as the rich young ruler's heart was not revealed until he heard the gospel — then it became clear that he loved riches more than God.

I hope so much that you can take in what I am saying here, because I believe it would show you my heart towards you and give you the needed understanding to bring healing to our relationship. I cannot deviate from the words of our Master that are recorded for us, for we live by every word that came and comes out of His mouth. The whole emphasis our Master was getting across in Matthew 10:34-39 is what following the true Messiah as a disciple will cause. There is a difference between the true Messiah and the false one, as 1 John 5:20 says,

---

[35] Luke 12:51-53

speaking about being in the real Messiah, since there are so many false ones being propagated by Christianity.[36] The whole letter of 1 John talks about what it means to be in Messiah and to have eternal life. So if a person lives out and practices what it says in this letter, he can know that he has passed out of death and into life, because the Holy Spirit in him will give him that witness.[37]

The gospel kills our old man so that we can live a new life. The Holy Spirit cannot do His work in us unless He can make His home in us. This is why the gospel is preached, and it is through the proclamation of the gospel that faith comes to a person.

The first church that started in Jerusalem at Pentecost developed into the twelve tribes of spiritual Israel.[38] However, by the time the letter of James was written, the twelve tribes had a false faith,[39] because faith without works is dead.[40] No longer was the gospel they preached valid, since no sent ones were available to preach faith to anyone. In other words, they no longer lived what they preached. The narration didn't match the play. The church died since the false gospel could not put an end to anyone's old life that they might live a new life in Yahshua.

Do you think God would entrust His Spirit to a fool? A fool is a person who is fooled by the false gospel, or who is foolish enough to believe a lie. A fool is a person who believes that Messiah's work alone is

---

[36] 2 Corinthians 11:4; Revelation 18:2
[37] 1 John 3:14,24
[38] Acts 26:7; 1 Peter 2:9-10; Titus 2:14; Revelation 1:5-6; 5:9-10; 21:9,12; Ephesians 2:12; Galatians 6:16; James 1:1
[39] James 2:14-27
[40] James 2:18-20

enough to save him apart from his sincere response by a death corresponding to His, or without true repentance in doing what is necessary to be worthy of Him, as the gospel teaches in Matthew 10:37-39.

This means that no one can be saved by Messiah's death without faith, because without faith no one can obey the demands of the gospel. To try to do it without faith would be just legal obedience. This is the reason why Christians persecute those who do have faith, because their faith exposes the fact that Christians merely have a principle of faith, but not true self-sacrificing faith. This faith is only imparted by the Holy Spirit upon hearing the gospel from a sent one, as in John 7:17-18.

A sent one is a person who is actually sent by God Himself. He seeks the glory of God and brings a gospel that exalts Yahshua, causing those who receive that gospel to make Yahshua their Sovereign and to give up everything for His sake. Someone who is seeking his own glory is not sent by God. He is sending himself. The gospel that he brings does not exalt Yahshua and cause those who receive it to make Yahshua their Sovereign, giving up everything for His sake. But only if a person is willing to do God's will can he know whether what he hears is actually from God or is just from the one who speaks, because one gospel is true and the other is false. One person proclaims the true gospel and is blessed; the other person proclaims another gospel and is cursed.[41]

Right now His true disciples are betrothed to Him, being prepared for marriage. He has so much

---

[41] Galatians 1:6-9; John 7:18

to say — so much must be revealed to us before the end. God has not spoken one word to Christianity for about 1,900 years. Ever since the candlestick of the first-century church was blown out, He doesn't walk among them anymore. They just live on the memory of when they once were alive. So now they just recite different creeds — the Apostle's Creed, the Nicene Creed, and so on. In the liturgy it's all planned and written out for them, even weeks in advance, including the sermon and which page in the hymnal to turn to.

Yes, there are many people in Christianity who are very sincere in wanting to love God and serve Him, and He will make sure that they will be confronted with the true gospel, just as you have been. And if they are willing, they will respond to the words of life they hear. It will actually be what they are longing for. It will not be just nice words they hear, but there will be a demonstration of life to back up the words. Yes, the life of the next age, when Yahshua will rule over the whole earth, has to be expressed as a foretaste and a witness in this age, as Matthew 24:14 says. And it will be expressed as that witness in all the places where Yahshua rules now.

So you can see what God has to do and what He's doing now before His Son can return to the earth. God is establishing His kingdom on earth now in this age as a foretaste. The restoration of the people of God has to take place first before Messiah can come back. Acts 3:21 must happen, but first Mark 9:12 must happen. First things first. It is just as in the Old Covenant when Elijah came to bring restoration to

Israel. At that time, there was hardly any difference between Israel (who were supposed to be the people of God) and the nations around them. Actually, there really wasn't any difference. They had fallen so far that they didn't even know who the true God was until Elijah came and brought that revelation back into Israel. However, Elijah only restored an altar of twelve stones, not a nation of twelve tribes. But it was prophetic of the restoration that would take place in the latter days, in fulfillment of Isaiah 49:6.

To those who have eyes to see, this restoration is taking place now, this nation that is being formed, and it is marvelous in their eyes. They are being called to participate in the restoration of the Body of Messiah.[42] The Body, when restored, will be exactly as Ephesians 4:1-16 and Philippians 2:2-4 describes, meaning that every member of the Body is giving his full potential — all he is and all he has — to the building up of the Body of Messiah, the Community. This is what love is, and this is what it means to be led by the Spirit.

This means that every person in the Community will be functioning with the glorious power of God and His grace, having wisdom and understanding and the true knowledge of His will. This is the only way someone can walk in a manner worthy of Yahshua and please Him in all respects and bear fruit in every good work.[43] This means that every person will walk just as Yahshua walked, and love as He loved.[44] The result of that is the unity of faith.

---

[42] Ephesians 4:1-6,16
[43] Colossians 1:9-11
[44] 1 John 2:6; John 13:34

This unity is the expression of having received the glory of Yahshua, the love of God that has been poured out by the Holy Spirit into the heart of every true believer. As our Master prayed in John 17:21-23, love is always expressed in unity, because love is the perfect bond of unity.[45]

Sounds utopian? But remember, it has already happened as recorded in Acts 2 and 4, and remember, there is going to be a restoration of that according to our Master's own promise in Mark 9:12. It's going to startle the whole world some day. Love is what is going to startle the world. Some people can see it, and some can't. It's all according to a person's heart. The world doesn't know what love is. Luke 12:49-52 is the fire that will light up the whole world soon, which is now being kindled by such love for Messiah as shown by ransoming my own life, or sacrificing my own self-life for His life to become that fire in me.

By His grace and strength I want to endure in this precious life and pass it on to our children. It's all that I have to offer them of any value, that they would love God and love one another at any cost. We want to teach them to do the will of their Creator, to be kind, to share, and to give — to possess these qualities that, unlike material possessions or comforts in life, can't be taken away. These things are eternal[46] — only what we build between each other and our God will remain.

Our Master said in Luke 6:24 that the only comfort some people will receive for all eternity will

[45] Colossians 3:14
[46] 2 Corinthians 4:18

be what they have in this life.[47] I would rather be like the poor man who, when he died, was carried away by angels to a place of comfort, than the rich man or the Christian who pretends to see when he is not doing as Abraham did[48] — because those who pretend to know Him and do not keep His commandments are liars and the truth is not in them.[49] It's an awesome judgment that their guilt will remain forever and ever, according to Revelation 19:1-3. I don't want my guilt to remain.

You know, there is something that is becoming very clear to me over time, and is now very much on my conscience, and that is how I have failed you many times in having wisdom and understanding and being filled with His love in representing this life to you.

We have been learning a lot about Exodus 20:5-6 — about the sins of the fathers being passed on to the children to the third and fourth generation. Have you ever thought about what those sins or inherited tendencies are that have been passed on to you from grandma and grandpa and the generations before? I know I have thought a lot about it. I remember writing a letter telling Grandma how sorry I was for getting so angry at her one time. She wrote back and so lovingly forgave me. She said, "You know, honey, it comes from both sides of the family." Some of my deep besetting sins are becoming clearer to me, as community is designed to bring it out — anger,

---

[47] 1 Timothy 6:9
[48] John 8:39-47, as John 9:41 says
[49] 1 John 2:4

anxiety, selfishness, strife to get something when I want it, stubbornness, among other things.

Anyway I know I am responsible for all these inherited tendencies and deep moral disorders that have been passed down to me, and I see there is no way for me to be delivered from them except that Yahshua would save me, and it's only in His Body — the Body of Messiah where true forgiveness is — that I have the hope to change.

I am thankful to live in this place where I can practically live out His commandments[50] and do His will[51] and be set free from all the bent ways in me, many of which I have inherited from you. You cannot honestly say that you or any of my own brothers or my sister has been set free and will not see death, being set free from these inherited iniquities in us, these evil bent ways, mannerisms, and temperaments which can only be healed by living in the healing environment of the Body, the Community.

Yes, the Community is the perfect environment to be healed, because living like this causes you to face what is in you — all your selfish ways and other manifestations of self-life. But we are not without hope, because it is possible with the help of Yahshua, by the power of His Holy Spirit, to put to death the old man with all of his iniquities and corruptions — all the things in us that hinder us from keeping the commandments of God, and to live a new life in Yahshua with the power to love.

This is not an easy life, and it was never meant to be. It is called "the narrow way." This is what it means

[50] John 14:21
[51] Matthew 7:21

to pick up your cross daily, which is the only way to follow Yahshua. But there is nothing more satisfying and fulfilling than to experience fellowship with your Creator, having His love and approval because you are doing what you were created to do.

The sad story, however, is that although the first-century church started out with this life, they didn't endure in it. Many in the church became enemies of the cross of Messiah.[52] Many started pursuing their own desires, thus falling into the snares of the devil, being held captive by him to do his will.[53] They eventually turned the whole church into a prison of unclean spirits, as Revelation 18:2-5 chillingly describes.

So that's why I plead with you now to come out of her and be washed of your sins, which have piled up as high as the skies — all these inherited tendencies that will bring you to death. Come out before it's too late, for the day will come when she will be judged for all her sins,[54] because she claims to see when she really doesn't. This judgment will happen, but it will be after you are no longer living. However, we can be those who endure to the end of this age,[55] to even have our lives prolonged in order to carry out His will, His good pleasure, and be purified. We have this hope because Matthew 1:21 promises that His special people will be saved by Him from these bent ways that cause us to hurt others.

When I say "special people," it's not that we are so special naturally, for we are just the outcasts and

---

[52] Philippians 3:18
[53] 2 Timothy 2:26
[54] Revelation 18:5,8
[55] Matthew 24:34; Isaiah 53:10

misfits of society — the "not many noble" that Paul spoke of in 1 Corinthians 1:26-31. Remember? So anyone can fulfill the qualifications to become a chosen one, because God chooses the foolish and weak things, the base and despised things, the things that are nothing in the world. The point is that only the ones who see themselves as fitting this description can see their need for salvation and are desperate enough to respond to His call. The ones who respond to the call are the chosen ones. Many are called, but few are chosen. So you see, it's not that we are so special, but it's that our God is special. He has qualified us.[56] We just obeyed the royal invitation.

So you see that the people of Yahshua, who are the ones He is going to save from their bent and crooked ways, have a hope which nobody else has ever had. This hope is to be different. Apart from this hope, people all die with their inherited tendencies. No matter how much they wanted to change and not be like their mothers and fathers, they couldn't escape it. I am thankful that, as I come to see my sins and confess and forsake them, He is faithful to forgive me and heal me.

I want to love the way God loves. I want to be pure in heart and pure in my motives in whatever I may say to you concerning the good news that I received. For I know the words of life that I heard when I came to Chattanooga were spoken from a pure heart and a good conscience, as well as from a sincere love for the brethren.

---

[56] Colossians 1:12

Being with them, with the ones who are just like those described in Acts 4:32-37, is the only way I have come to know faith.[57] This faith caused me to obey the demands of the gospel as in John 3:36. If I had disbelieved the gospel and rejected it by not obeying it, I would be judged already as in John 3:18.

Saints means "holy people," and holy means "set apart." The holy in Revelation 22:11 were made holy as God is holy. To be holy or set apart for God and His purpose, one must be ransomed. We had to set ourselves apart by obeying the gospel. The gospel tells us what God did in Messiah's sacrifice to save us from our sins. It also tells us what we must do to make ourselves worthy of Him who is holy. The gospel tells us about Messiah and His work for us, that we can now be saved from our sins[58] if we repent.

This word repent is not just a mental concept or attitude, as I said before. It means obeying the "many other words" as in Acts 2:38-41. Although these many other words are not spelled out in Acts 2:38-41, the result makes it clear what Peter told them. These many other words were the ones the Master commanded the apostles to teach them in Matthew 28:19-20, as you can very easily ascertain by the subsequent response and life of those who received his message, as described in Acts 2:42-47 and 4:32-35. Up until they heard these words, they were only cut to the heart and they asked what they should do. So Peter, with the rest of the disciples, told them what they were commanded to teach — as Matthew 28:19-20 says very plainly. Unless

---

[57] Romans 10:17
[58] Matthew 1:21

people know what to do, they can't do it. So the good news tells us what to do, what it takes for the repentant person to have eternal life and be entrusted with the Holy Spirit — that he must also make a corresponding sacrifice of his own life.[59]

They had to be tested to see whether they were now willing to do His will and be baptized, that is, to die with Messiah in His death as Romans 6:2-5 says, so as to live a new life in the Body.[60] The many other words in Acts 2:39-41 told about that which Messiah had commanded them. If one does not include this in the gospel, then he is accursed. The last instruction of Yahshua to His apostles before He ascended to heaven was to "make disciples, teaching them to obey all that I have commanded you."[61]

How else could the disciples they made confess openly that Yahshua is Sovereign and has first place in everything[62] unless they knew the good news about Luke 14:26-33, especially verses 31-32 about the Sovereign King Yahshua who is coming.[63] It will be only the faithful followers who are loyal to Him, who walk worthily of Him, who will be taken up to meet Him in the air.[64]

Only the righteous will inherit the kingdom of heaven (His reign on the earth in the next age), and yet I am not righteous in the way I am sometimes — this is the problem. Please don't misunderstand me.

---

[59] 2 Corinthians 5:14-15
[60] 1 Corinthians 12:13
[61] Mark 10:28-30; Luke 14:33; Matthew 10:37-39; John 12:25-26
[62] Romans 10:9
[63] Revelation 19:11-20
[64] Revelation 17:14; Matthew 25:1-13; 24:29-31,40,41

I am thankful that I already have eternal life. By His blood and by His righteousness I have passed out of death and into life, because the blood of His righteous sacrifice has justified me. But in Yahshua I have the hope that one day I will be made righteous enough to enter the Kingdom in the next age with Him — that He could say of me, "Well done, good and faithful servant. Enter into the joy of your Master."

Ephesians 4:1-3 says how we serve in the one Body by the one Spirit, all having the same hope of our one calling, so now we must prove worthy of our calling. I desire to have wisdom and understanding, to know His will so that I could please Him in all aspects, and walk in a manner worthy of Him so that He will not have to tell me, "Depart from me; you didn't do the will of My Father — you practiced lawlessness." If that is being told to us, it means that we are not worthy of the Kingdom.[65]

He is coming back for a whole people who have made themselves ready — those who have been walking with Him in white[66] — those who walked in the deeds that were prepared beforehand for them to walk in, deeds that built up the Body.[67] These are not lawless deeds initiated and carried out by mere human effort, because deeds like this tear down the Body. But these are lawful deeds initiated by the Holy Spirit and carried out by His power by those who are surrendered to Him. This is the Bride that He will return for, which according to Revelation 21:9-12 is the twelve tribes of Israel. Are you part of

---

[65] 2 Thessalonians 1:4-5
[66] Revelation 3:4; 19:7-8
[67] Ephesians 2:10; 4:16

one of these tribes now? Unless you are, then Luke 13:24-26 says that He will not know where you are from. Only if you are from one of these tribes that are being prepared for Him are you in His dwelling place, because the twelve tribes will be His dwelling place among the nations in all eternity.[68]

1 Timothy 2:8 commands "the men in every place to pray, lifting up holy hands, without wrath and dissension." Those who have no wrath or dissension between them are the brothers and sisters who dwell together in unity — the Community of God. "Every place" means every township or locality where He has caused His name to dwell in a people who are experientially one.[69] The same is true today. The Community of the Redeemed lives in the midst of the secular community as a light to it.[70] This community is a witness of His kingdom in every place. There is no division or denomination[71] in this community in any of the places where He dwells on earth today as it will be through eternity when His dwelling place (according to Revelation 21:3) will be, just as now, among the nations.

So, Mom and Dad, I want to be a living sacrifice for Him as Romans 12:1-2 demands, separated from the world,[72] and for His sake and for the gospel's sake I do everything I do, as the gospel commands in Mark 8:34-36 and 10:28-30. We are to spend all of our waking moments in doing what builds up the

---

[68] Revelation 21:3

[69] Malachi 1:11; John 17:21-23; 1 Timothy 2:8; 1 Corinthians 1:2,10,13

[70] 1 Peter 2:9-15

[71] 1 Corinthians 1:10,13

[72] 1 John 2:15; James 4:4; John 12:2

Body and prepares the Bride.[73] We must do it in a worthy manner to Messiah Himself.

As a human being — a man — He had no advantage over us to walk as He walked, otherwise the Holy Spirit could not command us in 1 John 2:6 to walk as He walked. We have the same Holy Spirit as He did, and being forgiven by His blood, we have the same access to the Father and to His grace as He did. To say anything different is in effect to deny that Yahshua came in the flesh, which is the spirit of Antichrist. Therefore we are to walk in a manner worthy of Yahshua, lest we stain our garments and commit a sin unto death, a sin that would disqualify us from ruling with Him in His kingdom in the next age.[74]

Not that we would lose eternal life. Yahshua gained that for us when He paid for our sins with His death, and we made ourselves worthy to receive this great gift when we obeyed the gospel and forsook everything for His sake. But if we now don't live and continue to live our life in a manner worthy of Him by walking as He walked, we will have to spend the thousand years of the next age, when the glorious kingdom of Yahshua will fill the whole earth, in death, full of regret, weeping and gnashing our teeth.

So this is why I gave up my life to Him, as a ransom, for something of greater value than my own individual, short-lived, useless existence on this earth in this age. And this is why I give up my life for Yahshua's and the gospel's sake every day. And this is eternal life, to know the Father and the

---

[73] Revelation 19:7-8
[74] Revelation 3:4; Deuteronomy 21:22; 1 John 5:16-17

true Sent One from the Father.[75] We cannot know the Father except through obeying the gospel of His Son.[76] Just as when the rich young ruler asks in Mark 10:17, "Good Teacher, what must I do to inherit eternal life?" the answer of the Teacher is: "If anyone wishes to come after Me, let him deny himself, and take up his cross, and follow Me. For whoever wishes to save his life shall lose it; but whoever loses his life for My sake and the gospel's shall save it. Truly I say to you, there is no one who has left house or brothers or sisters or mother or father or children or farms, for My sake and for the gospel's sake, but that he shall receive a hundred times as much now in the present age, houses and brothers and sisters and mothers and children and farms, along with persecutions; and in the age to come, eternal life." That is the word of Yahshua, the Son of God Himself, as recorded in Mark 8:34-35 and 10:29-30. This is the gospel I received.

So now I have the Son, I have the life He promised,[77] and not to be disrespectful, I would dare you to read the letter of First John to see whether you have eternal life or not, for you may just be a Gnostic yourself and not a true follower of Messiah. This letter by John was written to believers or supposed believers to combat Gnosticism. And so, as 1 John 5:13 says, a person can judge himself by everything that is written in this letter and thus know whether he is a true believer and whether he really has eternal life, or whether he merely has some kind of mental

---

[75] John 17:3
[76] John 3:36
[77] 1 John 5:12

belief without the works that accompany true faith. Such a mental belief is the modern-day Gnosticism.

I hope that you can receive the royal invitation to participate in the eternal purpose of God by becoming one of His offspring who will faithfully carry out His will.[78] It's all a matter of being willing. "His bond servants shall serve Him, and they shall see His face, and they shall reign forever and ever."[79] This is the promise for those who accept His royal invitation and who endure by His grace and by His mercy to the end, giving their bodies as a living sacrifice.[80] We are already forgiven in advance of Messiah coming to earth as a man, even before the foundation of the worlds, in eternity past — but only if we are the ones who give themselves up into His hands in the Body in baptism is His forgiveness appropriated.[81] It's only the seed of Abraham who have faith and walk as Yahshua walked.[82]

Well, goodbye for now. I hope that you will honestly consider these things. Although I tried to be as clear, thorough, and concise as I could, I know what I've written to you has still amounted to a lot, and it might raise more questions in your minds. Please feel absolutely free to ask me anything pertaining to this letter, or to clarify anything where greater clarity is needed.

It's only out of love that I write to you.

—Kirsten

---

[78] Isaiah 53:10
[79] Revelation 22:3-5
[80] Romans 12:1
[81] 1 Corinthians 12:13
[82] Galatians 3:27-29; John 8:39-47

ABOUT THE AUTHOR

Kirsten is pictured here, with her husband Martin and six children. In spite of her two kidnappings, she continues to be an example of loyalty and faithfulness to those who have known her during her 30 years as a member of the Community.

She holds no bitterness towards those who were instrumental in arranging and carrying out her two kidnappings. She has only written this story after 25 years of consideration and reflection in hopes that it will shed some light on the motives of those in the anti-cult movement who continually raise the specter of a "cult scare" for their own ends and gain, without consideration for the sincere and deeply held religious beliefs of those whom their actions directly affect.

Rebecca Westbrooks in 1980

APPENDIX

THE KIDNAPPING OF REBECCA WESTBROOKS

The true story of one woman's encounter with Ted Patrick and the degrading and deceitful tactics used to deny her the freedom to practice her religious beliefs.

January 17, 1980, Chattanooga, Tennessee

Around 3:30 pm, the police came into our office on McCallie Avenue, saying that they had a warrant for my arrest. The charge was possession of marijuana for resale. All they said was, "Stand up and put your hands behind your back." They handcuffed me and took me out to the car.

On the way out, the city detective asked me, "Have you ever seen this man?" He called the man "Mr. Myers."

I said, "Never."

He said, "That's not what Mr. Myers says."

They took me to the police station on Amnicola
Highway. A police woman searched me, and then
I was handcuffed to a chair and left alone. After a
few minutes, the detective came back and read me
my rights, then left me alone again for several more
minutes. He then came and took me to the city jail
downtown. I gave information about myself and
was told I could make one phone call. I called the
Community and asked Gary Long to have someone
come quickly. He said Judy and Arthur were getting
money for my bond and were on their way.

The detective came and asked whether I was
detective Westbrooks' daughter. He then seemed
apologetic and said he would take care of the bond. I
told him it was okay, that either I or my friends would
take care of it. I was then taken to the back where mug
shots and fingerprints were taken. Then they wanted
me to sign my bond, but I saw at the top corner that it
was written, "Have her father sign." I then hesitated
and said I wanted to wait for my friends to come,
but the policeman said, "No, hurry up and sign. We
haven't much time." So I signed. They told me to be
in court at 3:00 on Friday.

I walked out the door and there was my father
with the man called Mr. Myers. I ran back in and
started screaming that I wasn't going with him. They
came in, my dad handcuffed me, and then he and Mr.
Myers dragged me out to the car, where Arny and
Timothy Mahoney (friends of my dad) were waiting.
They drove toward Red Bank to the Cherokee Motel
(owned by a friend of my dad). There, Mr. Myers got
out and we went on.

It was there that my sister and her husband began following us in her car. After being on the freeway for awhile, we took a back road which headed toward Centre, Alabama. A few miles from Centre, my dad stopped to let me use the restroom. They all got out and escorted me. When I was finished, I began to walk toward the car, but then took off running. A car was coming down the street, so I put out my thumb as I ran and started screaming. It stopped, but everyone got hold of me and threw me back into my dad's car. We went on to Centre, where Sara Mosely (Naomi Kelley's sister) and her husband, Ronnie, were waiting for us at a church yard. We then followed her to her house. They put me in a back bedroom where the window was nailed shut.

The only conversation I can remember that night was between me and my brother in law. He asked to talk to me alone for awhile. He told me that he didn't fully agree with this and didn't know about it until that morning. He said they were supposed to have gotten me that morning as I walked to work, but I hadn't walked. Ted Patrick was supposed to arrive the next day, but couldn't stay more than two or three days because he had to be in court Monday in California. My brother in law asked whether there was anything he could do. I asked him to call the Community and tell them what was happening. He told the deprogrammers that I asked him to call. They were upset and berated me for doing such a thing. Later he said that no one had answered when he called.

The next morning Naomi arrived, a deprogrammer and ex-community member who had been deprogrammed by Patrick. Then my mother came in with a girl whom she introduced as Sue, but in actuality it was Melinda Horton, another ex-community member who had been kidnapped and deprogrammed by Ted Patrick a few years earlier.

All this was hard for me because I had always trusted my family, but now I found them lying to me and betraying me and treating me as a criminal or someone insane. It hurt me deeply to know that now I could not trust them or be open with them as I always had before.

In the room, there was a king-sized bed. At night I had to sleep between Melinda and Naomi. There was also a twin bed in the room where someone else slept — sometimes my cousin, aunt, uncle, or Tim. At night, the bedroom door was also tied from the outside so that it could not be opened. Also, someone slept on a cot or mattress right outside the door. For the first three or four days, I wasn't allowed out of the room, and someone had to be in the bathroom with me whenever I used it or took a shower.

Naomi, Melinda, and Sara would talk off and on all day about the Community, especially about Gene. They would make jeering remarks about me, about my not talking, and the way I would just lie there. One time, Naomi got mad at me and started speaking loudly in my ear because I didn't show a lot of affection for my dad. The first couple of days, at times I would start crying and pray a little out loud, asking God to deliver me and help me not have bitterness in my heart. Whenever I did this they would start shaking me, telling me to stop, and would tell my mother that it was a form of self-hypnosis.

On the 12th day, Ted Patrick arrived along with his video cameras. He set up all his equipment, put two chairs in front of the camera and lights — one chair for me, one for him. He would talk and talk about how my mind had been reduced to less than a two-year-old. I had become a zombie, Gene Spriggs was a con man, etc.

I was not deprived of food or sleep, but considering the fact that I was taken against my will, locked up, and badgered with words, having everything that I believed in attacked, I felt as if I were fighting for my life mentally, emotionally, and spiritually. One thing that disheartened me most was when they said several times that if it took four months of my being there, they would do it. They would say the same things over and over again. One of Ted Patrick's noted statements was that the power of suggestion is root of all hypnosis. They said all they wanted to do was get me to think for myself. I told them I didn't object to this. I didn't want to be hypnotized or brainwashed by anyone. But the only way I was to prove this was by listening to the tapes they had on cults and read the books they had. So, I consented.

Before I was taken, I had seen a talk show on television where Ted Patrick was speaking. He said that in the deprogramming process he and his associates "snap the mind." When they have accomplished this "snapping," they can fill in whatever they want into that person's mind. This is how they deprogram someone. In the books I read during the deprogramming, it described the snapping sign as an emotional outburst.

On the 13th day this emotional outburst happened to me. All along I had prayed not to be bitter toward anyone. I remained calm and unresponsive to all the things they said to me. But on this day as I sat there on the bed and they continued to hammer me with the same accusations against the Community, and belittle me, I could handle no more. I began beating the bed with my fists and screamed over and over, "You want me to get mad, but I'm not, I'm not, I'm not!" It was strange for me, because as I was screaming, I was also thinking to myself that this is crazy. I'm telling them that I'm not going to get mad at them, but I'm mad and screaming at them.

It was as if I were two persons — on the outside screaming and uncontrolled, but my mind was totally sane. They smiled at one another, as this was to them a sign of my snapping. I had gone crazy, and now they could fill my mind with all the lies and accusations that had filled their minds. This was their intention, but I never received these things, because in my heart, I knew what I had experienced in my life, how God had led me to this people, and although they were not a perfect people, I knew that they had the same heart as I did — a heart which loves our God and only wants to do his will.

For these two weeks I would often lie in the bed at night, trying to think how I could escape, but finally I saw that the only way out was to go through it. So, on the 14th day I finally consented to go to what they call "Rehab" in San Diego, California. Ted Patrick, Naomi, and I were taken to the Atlanta airport where we flew together to California. Before leaving Alabama, they had me sign a "Power of Attorney" to my dad and write a note saying that I had been with my family for two weeks and was now on vacation with another girl. I asked why I had to do this. They said it was in case I wanted my dad to get my possessions from the Community. They didn't say anything about the note, but I assume it was for Ted Patrick's protection in case I took them to court.

We left Atlanta at about 1:30 in the afternoon. We arrived in San Diego about 10:00 pm. The first two nights, Naomi and I stayed at the Rehab house where Ted's daughter Ann lives. The rest of the two weeks, I was at the Rehab house down the road from Ted's, on Plato Drive. Both Rehab houses have iron bars on the windows and doors, which are locked at night. On Rehab, I could go to the beach, to Mexico, out to eat, to movies, to the zoo, etc., but I was not given any money at all. I was watched very closely, and Naomi was faithful to reinforce all the things they had said to me during the two weeks in Alabama.

All I heard day and night for that month's time was about cults, brainwashing, and hypnosis. They make it a point for all people on Rehab to see Dr. Dean's show — a famous hypnotist. Naomi, Maggie (another girl who works for Ted), Martin (a fan of Ted's), Arnie, Rhonda, and I went to see Dr. Dean. After the show, Martin talked to Dr. Dean, so he wanted all of us to sit down and talk with him. He, Martin, and Naomi mostly talked about cults and hypnotism. Arnie and I got up and walked around some. I didn't want to take any chances of being hypnotized.

They say that cults keep people in through guilt and fear. I honestly never felt any guilt or fear until I was taken. Over and over they talked about how much my family loved me, how they proved this love by spending thousands of dollars to get me out of a cult. They told me I had hurt my family so much, that my father was in poor health, and how he had stayed awake at night crying over me. They said that if I went back to the Community, I would be made to press charges against my dad. This was a tactic of trying to make me feel guilty for causing pain to my family through my involvement in the Community, and making me think the pain would greatly increase if I were to return. They were very skillful at using my emotional ties with my family to try and instill guilt that would keep me from returning.

So much I wanted to escape, but was afraid of being caught. One morning in San Diego, I got up enough nerve to get up earlier than anyone else (which I usually did) and call the Community in Chattanooga. I told Judy that I was coming home as soon as possible. I was so scared. I was shaking all over and could hardly walk. There were a few times when I possibly could have escaped, but I knew I would be taking great chances of getting caught, and then I didn't know what would happen. I found myself overtaken by fear — a fear that could have ruled my life forever if I had not truly known the

One who casts out all fear. I finally concluded that the only way out was to take the chance.

On Thursday, February 14th, exactly four weeks from the day I was taken, I was brought to the airport where a ticket to my sister's house in Texas was waiting for me. Naomi, Maggie, Arnie, and Rhonda took me there. Naomi gave me $80 that my mom had sent for me to buy clothes. At about 1:30 that afternoon they left me at my gate and went with Rhonda to hers (she was also leaving that day). My plane was to leave at 1:40, so I had only ten minutes.

There was a phone nearby, so I called Chattanooga. I didn't know what to do. It was the first time I had really been alone, and I wanted to leave for Chattanooga as soon as possible, but was still afraid of getting caught. So, I went ahead and boarded my non-stop plane to Houston. There my sister was waiting. We drove to her house in Beaumont. For those four weeks I had to suppress my feelings, thoughts, and everything inside me because I couldn't trust anyone. In Beaumont, my emotions began to emerge. I felt very fragile, that I would break at the slightest jar. I felt afraid of people. I knew that I had to get home as soon as possible.

So, the next day, while my sister was at work, I called the Community and told them I was leaving and would call as soon as I got to another place. I felt like I was breaking through a thousand barriers — two of which were guilt and fear.

There is no bitterness in my heart toward my family, Naomi, or Ted Patrick. The Lord answered my prayer. I had no desire to press charges. I only wanted to be free to live according to the convictions in my heart.

I believe that Yahshua has called us to live a life according to His teachings. I believe that my life in the Community is in accordance with these teachings. My hope in His mercy and faithfulness and my conviction that God spoke to my heart and led me to the Community were the only things that brought me through those four weeks. My earnest desire is to continue living according to these convictions.

January 1995

It's been fifteen years since I was taken in an attempt by my father to have me deprogrammed. Since my arrest by the police was just a means of getting me into the hands of the deprogrammers, I thought that the process of prosecution would end that day. However, I was wrong. They actually had planned to follow through with the process, take me to court, find me guilty, and put me on probation, where I would be under the covering of the state, needing to get a job and not go outside of Chattanooga. I would have to live with my parents, thus not be able to return to the Community. Since a deprogramming is usually accomplished in three days, they had a trial date set for me a few days after I was taken. But since I was not yet deprogrammed but still held in Alabama, they said I was sick and set another day for my case. That time I was also still not deprogrammed, so they said I was undergoing psychiatric treatment in a hospital and again set a new date for the trial.

But the third time I had already returned to the Community, so they proceeded with the hearing with me not present. The court found me guilty and sent a warrant for my arrest to the Vermont state police. Some brothers from the Community had actually gone to all three hearings and witnessed the lies that were said about the whole affair. Since I was being falsely accused and sought after by the police, it was impossible to let my family know where I was.

We hired an attorney in Chattanooga to look into the court record to try to expose the injustice that had happened to me in the court. We discovered one court order for a continuance of my case on which the presiding judge had scribbled a note to another judge saying, "Doug, this is the case of Detective Westbrooks' daughter that I told you about. He is having her deprogrammed in Alabama and she won't be here for the hearing." Upon finding out this information, one of the leaders in the Community went to one of the judges involved and confronted him with the conspiracy we had uncovered. Once the judge knew that we really knew what had happened, he ordered the court record expunged and the records destroyed.

By this time I was living in one of the communities in Germany. Once my name was cleared, I was able to communicate with my family again, and this made me very happy. However, my father's attitude toward the Community never changed. Because of this, I could never fully be restored to him. Although I was able to tell him on the phone that I forgave him shortly before his death three years ago, I never saw him after the deprogramming in Alabama.

Two and a half years ago, my mother and two sisters came to Europe to see me. It was the first time in the fourteen years that I had been in the Community that they had ever come to see for themselves the life that I had. They came a little apprehensive, but it wasn't long before they saw that all the things they had heard were wrong. They saw clearly that my husband loves and cares for me, that the children are happy, healthy, and much loved, and that everyone in the Community are normal people and not brainwashed, hypnotized zombies.

My mother said that now she saw what I had been trying to tell her for fourteen years. My sister now gets so angry to think of all the lies that she had heard and believed about us. She sees that the result of believing those lies was that our once close relationship was broken, and undue harm came both to me and my family.

As we took them to the train station for their return home, they said that they were sorry that my father had never come to see, because if he had, they know it would have been different with him. I am so thankful for this visit, that now my family can have peace about my being here. I felt like I had been fighting a battle for fourteen years and the battle finally ended.

—*Rebecca Westbrooks Tlapak*

JAMES CASE'S
DEPROGRAMMING

My parents invited me home for three or four days for a family reunion. My father's relatives were all going to be there to celebrate my grandmother's birthday. I came with my brother, who lives in New Hampshire, to spend the weekend with my family, and just as I expected, my grandmother had a birthday cake and all the normal, customary things. Then, when the weekend was over, most of my relatives all went home and I was presented with a bit of a surprise.

As I was getting breakfast my parents said they wanted to talk to me about my decision to join the Community (two and a half years before), and they hoped I would listen to what they had to say. So I agreed, and we sat down at the table. In the past, my parents hadn't had a whole lot to say about it. They had asked questions and wanted all the literature I could send them, so I sent them as much as I could so they would know where I stood with the Community. I labored in many letters and conversations to communicate to them what we believe, and about the life we live. My parents had visited, at least once together, and five or six times my mother came by herself, but they never stayed with us in our houses. They would come for a gathering or two, and supper, but they never really experienced our life. I really had a desire to communicate to them what our faith was all about, and what our Master had called us to do, so I saw this as a good opportunity when they asked to sit down and talk about it.

My parents started the conversation by saying that anytime you make a big decision in your life you have to really be sure of what you're doing, especially when it's a life-long commitment. They felt that in order to make the decision that I made, I should have researched the Community more extensively. Specifically, they felt that I should have checked with former members and critics of the Community to see what they had to say. They thought I should have looked in libraries, on the Internet, and anywhere else I could find information on the Community, so I would have all the sides of the picture and could make a rational choice, instead of doing something based on hearing only one side of the story. They felt like I had gotten myself into something that I didn't really understand — that I was tricked. If I just sat down and gave them 72 hours of my time, they felt like I could make a rational decision about the Community, once and for all. Unless I did that, I wouldn't really know for sure what the Community was all about. I wouldn't have all sides of the story, so I wouldn't be able to make a rational choice.

I told them that I was leaving tomorrow, and they had known that all along, so they should have started this 72-hour process two days ago. I said, "I'll go ahead and give you today, because I was already planning to be here today. What do you want to talk about? Let's go ahead and talk about it."

They had a bit of an argument about that. They really wished that I would go ahead and commit to it, but I wasn't willing. So they said, "Okay, let's not spend all our time arguing about it. Let's go ahead with what we said we were going to do."

They started describing to me the research they had done about the Community, how they researched on the Internet, checked with critics and former members of the Community in order to have the information they needed to understand what I was doing with my life. They tried to make me feel like I really needed to have this "information about the Community," in order to make this choice. They asked if I would talk to a critic of the Community, an expert on the Community. So I asked, "What, do you have him here, today?"

"Yes."

"Really, and you never told me?"

"No, we knew you wouldn't come if you knew."

They said that if I really had faith, then my faith would stand. I said, "Well, bring them on. I'll talk to them."

So they brought in Steve Hassan, whom they had paid to come down from Boston to counsel me. Twenty years ago he had left the Unification Church and become what he called an "exit counselor." He's written a book or two and has a lot to say about mind control, specifically about the mind control used by the Unification Church on him, and other groups he considers himself knowledgeable about, including the Community.

So, presenting himself as an expert, he sat down to explain to me what he had gone through twenty or so years ago as a college student being approached by the Unification Church. He painfully labored to explain how they had deceived him and led him astray through the doctrine and information he was given, and by not giving him the whole story about what they were doing. He said they gradually brought him into more and more knowledge about the Unification Church, using fear and making him feel like if he went elsewhere looking for information, it would mean he was going to be influenced by Satan. So they convinced him that he needed to believe what they said, and do what they said, even to the point of believing that Sun Myung Moon was the Messiah, and that his word was the word of God, and that what he said to do was what God was telling him to do. It was indisputable and infallible, and if anyone spoke out against it he was of the devil.

So his implication was that it wasn't really his fault, but that he had been led astray, he had been tricked. So having been tricked as he implied, he later found his way out of the Unification Church. He was in a car accident after having been one of the main leaders of the group. While he was in the hospital from the car accident, apparently his sister contacted him. He agreed to stay with her while he recovered, because of his inability to function, which would have caused other members of the Unification Church to have to take care of him. So instead of taking them away from the Unification Church he saw it as an opportunity to let her take care of him, and let these other members go about doing the business of the church — "God's will," as he said.

While he was living with his sister, his father found out that he was there, and within five days his father had woken him up to the reality of what he was doing, and he was able to recover from this mind control that he claimed to be under. He went on to describe the way mind control works, and how it was used by the Communist Chinese and other groups. He described how people can be led into things, tricked and fooled into giving away their own conscience and their own free will, and how it wasn't their fault that they had done this, but they were under a fear tactic used by these so-called mind-controlling people.

Then he went back to the topic my parents had started with, about how I couldn't have made a rational choice about the Community apart from hearing both sides of the story, specifically critics and former members of the Community. He asked, "Have you ever talked to a former member of the Community?"

I said, "Yes, I've talked to a few."

"Anyone who was in leadership? Anyone who was an elder or an apostolic worker in the Community?"

"No, I haven't ever talked to anyone who was one of those and then left."

So he said, "Well, then you haven't really heard the whole story because you've never even been to an elders' meeting, have you?"

"No, I haven't been to an elders' meeting."

"Would you be willing to talk to someone who has?" It was all up to me, of course. "Would you be willing to talk to a former leader of the Community, someone who was in the Community from the beginning, an apostolic worker, community coordinator, and then later left the Community?"

And so, once again, I considered it, saying to myself, "If my faith is really faith, then it will stand. Our God is not going to let me be deceived. He won't give me more than I can handle. If I'm really willing to do His will, then I'll know the teaching, whether it's from God or whether it's from men." So with all compassion towards my parents, hoping they would believe me if I endured some of this for their sakes, I said, "Yes."

So they brought in Roger Griffin. He was very nervous and immediately left again to get some fresh air and a glass of water, came back, and went on to describe his life in the Community for 18 years: His father was a Baptist minister, and the reason he came to the Community was that they were a really good group of people who really wanted to do God's will and who really wanted to be *real* Christians. They weren't like the rest of Christianity. There was something different about them, and he liked that. He said that Elbert Spriggs (Yoneq) told him that he would be an apostle, and that there would be other apostles raised up eventually.

Roger went on to say that since Yoneq never raised up any other apostles, the Community was then under the headship of one man who had no checks and balances on him. He described Yoneq as one whom no one was willing to speak up against in cases where he was wrong. He implied that Yoneq used fear to intimidate people and keep them from speaking out against him if he made a mistake. And since he used this fear, and since he was very much in charge of everything the Community did, he eventually led the Community astray and into Old Testament legalism, into mind control, into deception.

This was very strange to me because what he described about authority in the Community was not what I had experienced over the last two and a half years. I had seen many men in authority who had much love and care for me and others, and whom Yoneq trusted to make decisions, and supported their authority in the Community.

Roger went on to describe a lot of personal things that happened to him that proved to him that the authority in the Community was bad, and that Yoneq was using mind control and fear to control people. What he said was in contrast to what I had experienced. I could see that he was deeply offended and was reacting to his offense by blaming Yoneq and the Community.

What I saw through it all was that he was accusing us of using fear tactics, but he himself was the one who really was using the fear tactics — he and Steve Hassan. I had spent about three hours talking to Steve, and about three hours talking to Roger. I saw right off that there was no use fighting back, arguing, or trying to convince them that they were wrong. It wasn't going to do any good. My only hope in staying and listening to them was that my parents would feel a little less fear about what I was doing with my life.

At about 6 pm, my parents said it might be a good time to break for supper. So I said to them, "Well, you've really given me a lot to consider." I made a very special point not to give any indication as to whether I was receiving them or not. I didn't want them to think I was receiving them, but I didn't want them to think I wasn't receiving them. I didn't want to be deceptive, but neither did I want to start an argument or have them lay into me. So I went out at that point, and said I was going to go for a walk and really consider the things they had said. "I need some time alone."

My parents live on top of a mountain in the middle of a forest. There is only one neighbor within three miles of my parents' house. About a quarter of a mile down a windy mountain highway there's a camping store right on the Appalachian Trail, with two pay phones, and the people who run it have always been good friends of mine. I went straight to the pay phone and called home to Rutland, reaching David Woodward. I asked him, "Do you think I should stay another two days for the sake of my parents, to put them at ease? Or should I just leave now?" He didn't think it was really necessary for me to stay, that I had heard a lot, and I agreed.

He said, "Tell you what, we'll get back in touch in about one and a half hours, so I'll have enough time to try and find transportation for you to get up here, and a way for you to escape." I could have just thumbed a ride, being right on the highway, but if they were going to find a ride for me, I thought it would be better to do that. So I went back to my parents' house.

I ate supper with my parents, Steve Hassan, Roger Griffin, and an old college friend named Tony, who was supposedly concerned for my safety, wanting me to get out of the Community for my own good, because he loved me, he said. My parents were obviously really affected by the fear tactics these men used, especially my mother who is normally prone to anxiety. After supper, I said I was going to take another walk and really consider these things, because I had really heard a lot and my parents knew it.

I called David, who said, "I've got a ride worked out for you. Your old friend Chris is willing to drive all the way from Atlanta to pick you up there. We told him you're having a little bit of a difficult time with your parents, and you need a place to go. He is willing to pick you up, give you a place to stay, and take you to the airport."

I called him and he agreed to drive the one and a half hours up to Georgia where my parents live and pick me up. Then I went back to my parents' house, considering what I would tell them on the way. For my parents' sake, I didn't want to just slip out the door. I wanted to be honest to whatever extent I could. They didn't hear me come in the door, so I went to my room and packed up my things. All I had with me was a backpack and a violin. I took them back through the house to leave, and my parents saw what I was doing, and were a little bit surprised, obviously. They asked me, "Where are you going? What are you doing?"

I said, "Honestly, I've heard a whole lot today, a lot to consider. I can't possibly take in more than I've already taken in. I'm going to go to Atlanta with an old friend of mine from college, where I can be free from the influence of these two men, free from the influence of the Community, on neutral ground, where I can consider what I've already heard. I will call you in the morning."

Their immediate assumption was that I was heading straight back to the Community. So they followed me out of the house, and on this quarter-mile walk back to the pay phone I continued to explain to them that they needed to give me the freedom to use my free will, because again and again they had talked about how it had to be a free-will thing. They said that obviously these religious groups, including ours, had taken away the free will of man and left him without a conscience, totally under the fear of their leadership.

My parents and Tony tried to physically keep me from making it to the place where I was going. In subtle ways they were getting in front of me and trying to slow me down. My mother was just racked with fear, crying and screaming and saying, "Oh no, I'll never see you again! You're going back to that place, and I'll never see you again!" She was under a blanket of fear. I could hardly even believe it. It was so thick. She was literally clinging to my clothes, trying to drag me backwards.

I just stood there and said, "Get a hold of yourself. Who here is really under fear? Am I?" This whole time I had been just lighthearted. I hadn't shown any signs of being afraid, as my parents expected me to be, of the information these men were going to give me. It was really clear who was under fear. "You know, I really feel betrayed by *you*!" I said to my parents. "These men are using the same techniques of mind control that they're accusing the Community of using. They used you to do this. First you brought me home, not telling me what I was in for. Then you brought out this man Steve, an "exit counselor," and then you brought out Roger Griffin — one step after another, a gradual release of the information that you had in store for me. This is the same technique this man described as having been used on him to lead him into the Unification Church."

My parents couldn't hear any of it. They had bought into these fear tactics, big time. By this time, it was about an hour before my friend from college would be able to make it there. I sat there with my backpack and my violin, and they continued to labor with me that I didn't know what I was doing, and to give them enough time to hear what they wanted me to hear so that I could make a rational choice. They said, "You're afraid to hear this information!"

Finally my friend Chris arrived. He didn't really know what he was getting himself into. He got out of the car, and he was surrounded by glares, and my mother refused to shake his hand. She was really suspicious, afraid that he was really someone from the Community. He said, "Look, I'm just here doing him a favor. I don't know anything about this situation." But no one would believe him.

Finally, we were able to make it out of there after they said one thing after another to try to convince us to stay. As we drove to Atlanta, I explained to him the kind of fears that were working in my parents, and how I couldn't even have a rational conversation with them. He didn't pry into it at all, but was just a true friend.

In the morning, I did what I promised my parents I would do. I read over the book, *Thought Reform and the Psychology of Totalism*, by Robert J. Lifton. I also looked over a collection of writings from a Stanford University college class about mind control. Steve Hassan had given me these two books, along with a Christian publication called, "Life in all its Fullness – The Word of God and Human Rights." Then I called my parents and said, "Well, I looked over this literature, and I considered the things you wanted me to consider, and I honestly believe that these men have really been lying to you and to me. They've been stretching the truth and leaving out facts in the stories they told, and they don't even know what they're talking about. They are hypocrites, using the same techniques they are preaching against, to convey their own personal agenda against the Community."

It was hard for my parents to hear that, but I told them I was going back to Vermont. They labored to keep me on the phone for as long as possible, passing me around from my mother, to my father, to Steve

Hassan, to Roger Griffin, to my friend Tony, and then back again. But I had heard them out, and now I had made my decision — that free-will choice they were telling me I was going to be able to make. I flew back to Vermont, and the next day I called my parents and told them I was safely home here in the Community in Rutland.

I'm really thankful for the opportunity to actually have the testing of my faith produce perseverance, and that as a result of this perseverance I could be perfect and complete one day, lacking in nothing. I'm thankful to be under the apostolic authority that calls a person to obey the truth as it says in Romans 1:5. It is a necessary thing for a person to be transformed into the image of Messiah. We are to not be conformed any longer to the pattern of thinking of this world, with all its sophisticated reasoning, but be transformed in our thinking by the renewing of our mind, as it says in Romans 12:1-2. This is what enables us to live in a way that proves to the world what God's will is.

I have come to find out that scholars in the field of social science and law have proven in court that mind control is a bogus theory that cannot be substantiated. What it comes down to is this: Who is Sovereign over the universe? Is it our Father, the Most High? Because if He is, then He is able to protect us — and anyone in the nations, all those born with a conscience — from being taken in by some deception. People are accountable to God for being deceived, since they did not cry out to Him for wisdom.

If someone leaves the Community telling horror stories about the mind control he was under, chances are he was living to please men and not God. He went on in the Community, having fallen away in his heart, darkened in his understanding, not giving thanks from the heart, not really seeking our Father. He is probably such a coward that he can't admit the real reasons he left the Community and resorts to blaming it on "mind control."

If we are afraid to speak what's in our heart for fear of being cast out because it might not agree with what authority says, then we're under some crazy religious demon and we need to repent and cry out for courage to do what's in our hearts, so that our obedience would be from the heart, not from principle or fear. I plan to continue to speak up against that kind of rote, ritualistic religiosity that I grew up in and finally left to come here, where it is exposed. Here, we who love authority and believe it to be from our Father can live in peace, and those who hate authority can find something easier to do with themselves somewhere else.

—James Case

JESSICA BARRETT'S
UNEXPECTED RECEPTION

Our sister Jessica in Boston went on a weekend visit home to her family. Once she arrived, however, she soon discovered that they had something more than a social visit in mind. Although they had visited our community, they remained fearful that their daughter might be in a cult. They called in the "professionals" to persuade her away from her faith. She stood firm in the truth of her faith and she spoke her heart.

After two days of their best efforts, they agreed on Monday to meet with some members of "her group." Sharon Brosseau, James Case, Stuart Lavin, and our friend Richard Robbins (Professor of Anthropology at SUNY in Plattsburgh), accompanied Jessica to her friend's living room. This is Sharon's account:

October, 1999

As we sat with Jessica's friends and relatives and with our opponents, preparing to respond to their questions, I noticed something. Jessica's mother and sister expressed their reasons for being there in a simple and sincere way. They were confused and concerned. But the opening remarks of the "exit counselor," Steve Hassan, showed a different motive. His experience as a former follower of Sun Myung Moon, his conviction that he'd been under "mind-control," and his years of studying psychology and mind control had given him complete confidence to judge us to be a "mind-control cult." He was not going to be moved by us speaking the truth. He was not going to hear anything with his heart.

As Stuart Lavin identified himself and spoke with compassion and wisdom to Jessica's mother, Mr. Hassan made critical and divisive remarks to the effect that Stuart had "become a good advertisement, a good piece of P. R. (public relations) for the Community." He wanted to intimidate and silence Stuart, and he wanted to disqualify him in front of Jessica's relatives.

At different times when Jessica made simple statements, he would draw attention to her words in a way that twisted the meaning and made it look as if she were oppressed and unable to think for herself. He was very practiced at planting thoughts in people's minds and powerfully directing them toward certain conclusions. He spoke with such self confidence, in such a condescending way, with such compelling reasoning, that others with less education might feel stupid for thinking differently.

Then, on the other hand, there were Bob Pardon and Judy Barba. They did not seem so intimidating, and came across as more down-to-earth type people. But they continually misrepresented our teachings, and did not listen when we gave answers to their questions. They, too, had their minds set. At one point they were even telling us what we believe, and they were quite wrong about it, but they would hear nothing from us. I finally said, "I cannot relate to what you are talking about. You may have read our teachings, but you do not understand what they are saying and you interpret them wrongly because you do not know the Spirit they are written in."

The main point they wanted to make, the primary lie they wanted to plant firmly in the minds of Jessica's relatives, was that we are dishonest about our beliefs, concealing things that might offend people, hiding the truth about ourselves. The questions they asked were like traps laid for us. They wanted to get any little phrase or sentence from our mouths that they could jump on and make us look like liars. What a difficult situation! They did not really deserve direct answers, since they did not want to hear the truth anyway. But Jessica's relatives wanted to hear – they could have appreciated an in-depth conversation that would have laid their fears to rest. But if we brought out our "pearls" in front of those other people, they would just trample on what we said and then tear us apart as a people and as individuals.

They had the familiar hostile questions: "Why can we not get straight answers from you people? Like this issue of leaders. For years many of you told us you don't have any leaders – no leaders. But you do have leaders! Why won't you tell us plainly about this? Why do you hide the fact that you have this big leader that's in control?" It was clear they had their minds made up about us and our "big leaders."

And there were the friends and relatives of Jessica, listening. I wanted to speak to them. It was no good trying to really answer those other people anyway. So I started, "When Messiah was on the earth, sometimes people would come to Him with questions. It could be really hard, because sometimes people who hated Him came with hostile questions. How was He supposed to answer them? If it was someone simple-hearted and sincere, like that woman at the well, He could just give them a clear answer like, 'I'm the Messiah,' because they really wanted to know. But if it was the other kind of people, that were trying to trap Him, He usually would not give a direct answer. Sometimes He wouldn't even answer at all, or He would turn it around and ask them a question instead."

Jessica's relatives sitting in front of me were nodding their heads in understanding.

"So when someone comes and asks us about our leaders, and you can really sense their hostility, it's very hard to answer. How do we talk to *them* about our leaders, who live with us and eat with us and serve us, people we love, who love us, who clean bathrooms or help us with laundry?

"Of course we have leaders! How could we function without leaders? But what is all this about leaders? Everybody has to be a leader. When Messiah left the first disciples and went back to heaven, He made them all leaders, because many more disciples were coming in to be built on top of them. And then those also had to become leaders, because even more and more were supposed to come in and depend on them. My children will grow up to be leaders. Jessica's growing to be a leader – she *is* a leader, you can tell!"

In Luke 7:29 after our Master spoke about John, it says that when all the people and tax gatherers heard it, they justified God, having been humble and needy enough to have received John's baptism. But the Pharisees and the lawyers rejected God's purpose for themselves, not having been baptized by John, who was making ready a people prepared for Messiah. Then there are verses 31-34, in which our Master talks about people such as Steve Hassan and Bob Pardon.

"To what then shall I compare the men of this generation, and what are they like? They are like children who sit in the market place and call to one another; and they say, 'We played the flute for you and you did not dance; we sang a dirge and you did not weep.' For John the Baptist has come eating no bread and drinking no wine; and you say, 'He has a demon!' The Son of Man has come eating and drinking; and you say, 'Behold, a gluttonous man, and a drunkard, a friend of tax collectors and sinners!' Yet wisdom is vindicated by all her children."

We just can't satisfy them, no matter what we say or do, because they are not needy, not looking for Messiah. The witness of the life goes right over their heads, they don't even see that they don't have it, because they are convinced that they already see (John 9:41). So what is there to say to them?

Our Master never would "sing or dance" on command. He never responded from pressure or from compulsion, to try to dispel someone's accusations. The humble and needy of the earth will justify God when they hear us and see the life of Messiah, because they will see and hear with their heart.

—*Sharon Brosseau*

Jessica's Report

I'm amazed at the stir my involvement in the Community has caused among my family and friends. They prepared a surprise meeting with me recently. Their stated objective was "to equip me with the necessary tools to make an informed choice to live in the Community." To help do this, they invited two women who left the Community (one of whom had been here for twenty years); plus Steve Hassan, a man recognized as an expert in helping people leave mind-controlling cults; Bob Pardon, one of the most vocal public opponents of our Twelve Tribes, and his colleague, Judy Barba.

Judging from the things that were said, my loved ones are apparently convinced that I live in bondage to an unscrupulous, rigidly hierarchical group controlled by a central leader who benefits from our labor; and that I am under forced submission and a victim of brainwashing.

Although I was not interested in "being equipped with tools to help me make an informed choice," I felt so sorry for their obvious neediness (especially my mother) that in hopes of representing our Master to them I submitted to their plan. (I had been tricked into participating in the meeting and was about three or four hours away from Boston.)

As time drew on, deceptive, unpleasant "information" was presented by these ex-Community "witnesses;" the others of my friends and family, ignorant of the deception, listened and asked questions. I still hoped to address my mother's fears, to bring her security, but for the most part I did not even respond with answers to these accusations. Obviously my mother (and the others) are pawns of the evil one, trapped in his kingdom, thinking the worst.

I was very thankful to be driven home to my covenant friends when the ordeal ended. The next day a few of us met with them, but they were still discussing doctrine and free will and various accusations. After a few hours it was obvious to me that my mother was not going to get peace. At one point different conversations had sprung up all over the room and no one speaker could be heard. I turned to my mother and asked her what she hoped to achieve by all this. She said she wanted me to know every fact there is to know about the Community, including what's written in all our teachings! Of course this was unattainable in our few hours. I told my mother after disorder had reigned for a time that I was leaving. My brother and sisters took me home.

What I learned from all this is how personally faithful our Father is. I had been praying for a long time to see how much I desperately need our Father, to be filled with His Spirit. What better answer than to put me in the perfect situation to represent Yahshua's love to those friends and relatives I care for with a deep longing? Though the pressure to believe lies about our God and our people was great I have confidence that because of grace I remained connected to the vine, not losing my peace, but even repenting when they pointed out some of my wrong ways.

I am thankful that the power of His overcoming Spirit was proven to me. I'm thankful to learn that when I am in desperate need He will not leave me desolate, for His kingdom's sake. I'm thankful to learn that powers and principalities cannot divide us from our Father's loving mercy unless we allow them to. I want my loved ones to be saved! I want, like so many who have gone before, to represent our Master's heart so that they will see that God owns our hearts, that a nation belongs to Him, that He is actively preparing His kingdom so that they will know they can be part of it too.

I know that grace abounds in every circumstance; all we need to do is humbly express our need and ask for help. I'm thankful that the bond between those who love Messiah goes deeper than family. We are connected through the blood relation of Yahshua, by an eternally enduring promise to love.

—*Jessica Barrett*

THE AMBUSH OF CHARLES BECKWOLD

January 8-10, 1999

Two weeks prior to my visit, I wrote my wife and asked her if it would be okay to come down on Friday evening so we could talk. On my previous visit in December she had said they were going to do a Bible study on covenants. So I thought this time when I went down on Friday night we could talk about what she was learning about covenants. She wrote me back the week before I went down and said Friday night was good, but to arrive after 6:00 because she didn't want me to be there while she was watching children.

By the time I got near Philadelphia the roads were pretty bad and I thought I would call my dad to see if he was home. If he wasn't at home, then I would just go straight to Ellen's. Even though I was a little early, I thought it might take me a little while to get there. It was 4:30 and she had told me not to get there until 6:00. I called my dad's and he was home. I told him since he was there I would come over and he said he would cook some leftover spaghetti for us. I got to his house and I noticed all the snow (he is 70 years old) and thought I would shovel the pavement for him so he wouldn't have to do it.

I called and my wife answered the phone and I told her I had just arrived after being on the road all day and that the roads were pretty bad and I was tired and would rather stay there and just come down on Saturday. Her voice kind of dropped as if she was really disappointed to hear I didn't want to come Friday night. She started trying to talk me into coming. She said, "Oh, can't you come? I sent the children to my sisters and I'm the only one here. Even if you're an hour late it's okay. Besides it's supposed to rain tonight and the roads are supposed to get really bad. So why don't you just plan on coming tonight and you can sleep over. Oh, don't worry, I'm not going to do anything."

I said, "I want to shovel my dad's pavement. I guess you prepared something for dinner." She said, "Yes, but that's all right. Even if you're an hour late it's all right."

I ate dinner at my dad's, shoveled the pavement, which took longer than I thought, and it was almost 8:00 when I arrived at my wife's. I showed up and it was really quiet. My wife said, "What do you want to talk about?" I said, "I was thinking about talking about covenants because you said you were going to do a Bible study about covenants a month ago and I want to hear what you're learning." So she went on to say that the Bible study teacher was sick and because of the holidays they didn't have a Bible study in the last three weeks. Then she looked at me and said, "You know how I've wanted you to talk to somebody for the last five years? Well, I was thinking, would you talk to somebody tonight? Would you do it for me?"

I said, "Why, are they here?" And she said, "Yes, they're at Nancy's house." So I said, "Okay." She made a phone call and about five minutes later Nancy came, and also Hank (a man who faithfully writes to me every other week). Then another man and woman came in, and I thought he said his name was Tom. He introduced the woman as Judy. He didn't give her last name, so all I remember is Tom and Judy.

He said he was from Massachusetts, and that he had known the Community for a long time. He said he knew Hakam, Racham, Ehud (he mentioned a lot of people in the Community), and he seemed to know them and said they knew him. He told me he really admired my stand, giving up my wife, children, and home for the Gospel. After showing a short film about a strange group, he went on and on about these groups and the way they were and how they see people. I remember stopping him in the middle of his conversation and telling him he might as well be speaking Spanish because I couldn't relate to anything he was saying. I said, "It's not that way in the Community. I can't relate to anything you're saying. I don't want to waste your time or ours."

He said, "Oh, I appreciate you speaking up." It was about 10:30. I ended up staying over and sleeping downstairs. At 8:00 Saturday morning we were just finishing up breakfast and my wife asked me if I would talk to an ex-member of the Community. I said, "Here in town?" She said, "Yes, he flew in." She said he came from somewhere in Tennessee. So I said, "Sure, I'd be glad to talk to him." I didn't know who she was talking about. She made a phone call and this woman Nancy shows up again with Hank and a man named Roger Griffin.

So we sat down and Roger started talking. He went way back to when the Community first started and he said, "Most of us were Christians and we belonged to a couple of fellowship groups." He said at one point Yoneq had cut this one fellowship group off. Roger said, "I had a lot of Christian friends in that fellowship and Yoneq just cut them off and didn't want anything to do with them anymore. But he didn't say why." He told me how Yoneq had all these plans for Tennessee — building cafés, raising up apostles, and lots of things. But Roger said it never came about. It never happened and we ended up leaving Tennessee and moving to Island Pond. I remember stopping him at that point and saying, "Roger, even though he had vision for Tennessee, these things still could happen. We're not even born as a nation yet. It could still happen. We're still small right now."

Then he went on again about how Yoneq said he was going to raise up apostles, but it never happened — just Yoneq. He was the only one. Everything came through Yoneq. I stopped him again and said, "Even though we don't see many apostles in the Community, they are being raised up. There are many of them functioning in their gifts. They're there in the Body."

Roger kept saying how Yoneq makes all the decisions in the Community. "No one can think on their own. We all have to agree with Yoneq." He asked me many times, "Where did Yoneq get his authority?" After he kept saying it so many times, I said, "It's amazing, but in Yahshua's time the Pharisees asked Yahshua where His authority came from." And I asked Tom, "Are you a Pharisee?"

Tom kept bringing up this verse in Acts 17:11 about the Bereans and how they searched the Scriptures daily to see whether these things that Paul was saying were true. He sort of associated himself with the Bereans; they were more noble and would search the Scriptures, and that was what he was doing. He was going to search the Scriptures and see if Yoneq was teaching according to them.

I remember Tom saying to me that he knew the teaching came from the anointing and it seemed he understood that unless he was under the anointing he wouldn't be able to understand the teachings. He also said he had many teachings from the Community. I remember Tom pulling out a teaching and we started to read it. I forget what it was, but it made me think about what the cost of being a disciple was. He said, "Oh, I'm glad you mentioned it; let's turn to that in Luke 14:26. Let's look at that." He said, "Ok, Yahshua meant it literally, 'If anyone comes to me and does not hate his father and mother, wife and children, brothers and sisters, yes, even his own life, he cannot be My disciple.' Then down a little further it says, 'You cannot be My disciple unless you give up all your possessions.' And the third one was, 'Whoever wishes to save his life will lose it, but whoever loses his life for My sake will find it.' So if you take the first two literally, then you have to take the third one literally. He's saying to die, but of course He doesn't want us to kill ourselves."

He was reasoning it away so I said, "No, He means you need to die — not take your life, but give up your life." I tried to explain to him that you can't come to know God by reading your Bible. I said, "You can read it and read it and read it, but you'll never come to know God. You may come to know a little *about* Him, but you'll never really come into a personal relationship with God. The only way you can come to know our Father is through receiving a disciple and receiving his message."

I remember telling him that the Bible was written to believers, not to just anyone. If you don't have the Holy Spirit, all the Bible can do is make you more confused. (I wanted to have compassion on this man. I didn't really know him and he seemed to be sincere at first, but the more he talked I could tell he didn't understand. I tried to explain it to him as simple as I could.) I remember telling him that faith comes by *hearing*, not by reading. It comes by hearing from a sent one. It's one thing to read about the cost of being a disciple, but it's another thing when our Father sends a disciple to you and he preaches the good news to you in person. Then you're confronted with the truth and you have to decide what you're going to do with it.

I told him how the very example of this is in Acts 13:42 where it says, "When the Jews went out of the synagogue, the Gentiles begged that these words be preached to them at the next Sabbath. And when the congregation had broken up, many of the Jews and devout proselytes followed Paul and Barnabas, who, speaking to them, persuaded them to continue in the grace of God. On the next Sabbath almost the whole city came together to hear the Word of God. But when the Jews saw the multitudes, they were filled with envy, and contradicting and blaspheming, they opposed the things spoken by Paul. And Paul and Barnabas grew bold and said, 'It was necessary for the Word of God should be spoken to you first, but since you reject it, and judge yourselves unworthy of everlasting life, behold, we turn to the Gentiles.'" I told him that it was a serious thing to not receive the message from the sent one, from a disciple. It has grave consequences.

Again, Tom would say, "No, the Bereans were more noble and they searched the Scriptures to see if these things were true." He said more than once, "If this were the truth, I'd be the first one to join the Community." I remember Tom saying that some things were already understood among the believers so they weren't written down. Then he started having a hard time again with living in community. He said, "You don't have to live in community to be saved."

I said, "That was one of the things that was understood by the believers. If a person believed in the Gospel from the sent one, and he obeyed the Gospel and gave up everything, he would find himself living with other believers with the same heart and the same mind. He would find himself living in community with other believers."

I remember telling him that Yahshua's prayer in John 17 was that the believers would be one even as He and the Father were one. "The covenant we make with one another as believers is greater than a marriage covenant in the world. I wouldn't know what it meant to be one if I hadn't been married to my wife, Ellen. I knew what it meant to be one, so when I read that in John 17 where Yahshua said, 'Let them be one just as the Father and Son are one,' I knew that this oneness had to be greater than a marriage covenant in the world."

I gave him another example in 1 Thes 2:8 where Paul says, "So, affectionately longing for you, we were well pleased to impart to you not only the Gospel of God, but also our own lives, because you had become dear to us." And then I told him in 2 Cor 7:3 that Paul said, "I do not say this to condemn; for I have said before that you are in our hearts, to die together and to live together."

I remember him saying, "Oh, God wants us to read the Bible and live by the principles of the Bible." I told him that the Gospels and the Epistles weren't self-help books. They weren't written so you could better your life or make the world a better place or help improve self. But the Gospels, when believed, will help you end your life (terminate it). I just wanted to make it really simple for him, but he just kept making it more complicated by his reasoning. I told him, "If Paul were here today you'd have a hard time with him, too."

We took a break for awhile and around lunch time a couple of my sisters showed up. I asked them what they were doing here. Then my father showed up from Philadelphia, and I was really surprised to see him. I said, "Dad, what are you doing here?" He didn't say anything. After lunch time there were about eleven people (some church friends of my wife dropped in, too) besides myself.

Tom wanted to share a video that he said was short. He said it was a true story where a teacher in his classroom did an experiment. Later he lost his job because of this experiment. So we all went downstairs and he put in his video and it starts out where the teacher is showing a film on the Holocaust. It showed the picture of Hitler. At the end of the film you see a lot of dead bodies and a lot of Jews are skinny and starving. It really affects the students in the class. One girl says, "Wow, how can one man have so much power? How could he get all these soldiers to carry out his will and kill all these Jews?"

So over the next few days the teacher puts the students through an experiment of becoming slavishly obedient to authority, first his and then whoever in the class draws the right card that day. One girl goes home and starts telling her mother about the experiment and the mother doesn't like the idea and tells her daughter she doesn't want her to be a part of it. So she goes in to class the next day and her boyfriend is in the same class. She confronts him and tells him she doesn't want to participate in this experiment and the boyfriend gets really mad at her and says, "You have to. You don't have any choice." And she says, "Yes I do. I'm not going to do it." The boyfriend tells her she just needs to find herself another boyfriend. She goes to her locker room and someone writes on her locker, "enemy" and she's really scared. During the week, even fights break out in the school and the classroom is chanting this chant and it really gets out of hand.

The next day there was a flag that was called the "wave" with a code on it that the students couldn't make out, but the teacher translated it and said, "The wave is upon us." He tells his class that they weren't the only ones who were experimenting, but it was a nation-wide experiment with a lot of other schools. He said there was a leader and at noontime they were going to go down to the auditorium and find out who this leader was. So at noontime the whole classroom went down to the auditorium and the teacher turned on two movie screens and there was a lot of static. The class sits there for about a half an hour and nothing is happening and they start getting fidgety and looking around. Someone says, "Mr. Smith, there's no leader. This is just a hoax." And the teacher says, "There is a leader," and he turns on the big screen and it's Adolf Hitler. He says, "This is the leader."

So Tom turns the TV set off and says, "History is going to repeat itself." And I said, "That's right, history is going to repeat itself. One thing this film failed to mention was that Adolf Hitler was a Christian and the 'wave' is Christianity. We're headed for a one-world government and a one-world religion. History is going to repeat itself; when Christianity and the

State are married there will be bloodshed. That's what we're coming into."

When he turned off the film I noticed that my wife was crying and it had upset my two sisters and a couple of the women. We talked some more and I remember that Roger was sitting next to me and he looked right at me and started talking to me. We looked at each other right in the eyes and he said in front of everybody (I won't use the exact words he did) that the Community had castrated me. He said, "You're not even a man. You can't even think for yourself. You can't even provide for your wife and children."

I said, "I've heard enough, I've seen enough, and as far as I'm concerned this meeting is over and I'm through talking." I said to my wife, "I want you to bring the children home tomorrow because I'd like to spend some time with them before I go back to Boston." So she said she would; that she'd make sure they were there. Then they started trying to talk me into staying. My father had left about a half hour before that and I told him, "Dad, I'll be along right behind you. Leave the light on." I remember my wife saying, "Oh, stay. Your sisters took off from work today to see you. Please stay." I said, "No, I don't want to stay."

I said goodbye and went outside and there were some cars in the driveway and I didn't know if I was going to be able to get out or not. I sensed that they didn't want me to leave. I really didn't want to go back into the house. I thought I could turn around although it was real close to the house. At one point

I knew I was going to have to go up on the lawn and I was hoping there was enough room between my car and a tree so I could get out. I was going to go for it because I could sense they weren't going to move the cars for me and they were hoping I couldn't get out. Somehow I managed to turn around and I zigzagged around a few cars and up on the lawn and I just made it. I was so thankful my car just fit through this little spot and I didn't have to go back into the house.

I went to my dad's and it was about midnight when I got there. I remember waking up three or four times and it was still dark. After the fourth time I got up and got dressed; it was 6:30 in the morning. I wanted to go see my brother in a correctional facility on the way to see my wife. I got there about 7:30 a.m. and visiting hours were at 8:00. While I was waiting I was hoping that Tom, Roger and Judy would still be at my wife's when I got there because I had something on my heart to tell them. That film had bothered me a little and how it had affected some of the other people in the room.

It was 9:30 when the guards told me I couldn't see him without a letter from the warden, so I left. On the way to my wife's house I was praying that our Father would give me boldness to speak what was on my heart, what I had thought about the whole weekend. I was praying that I would put a little fear into this man, Tom, because I knew that film put some fear into some of the people who were there watching it the night before.

When I arrived at my wife's house it was about 10:15 and my children were there and I greeted them.

Then I went right to my wife and said, "Ellen, I want to talk to you and Tom and Judy right now. Go down and tell them." So they came up and to my surprise Roger was there, too. We all sat down and Tom asked me, "What did you think about the video?" And I said, "It bothered me, and that's why I want to talk to you. The purpose of that video was to say that living in community was evil, and not only that, but that the community I live in is evil." I told him that he didn't have the Holy Spirit, and I said, "The Holy Spirit would never use a worldly video like that. All that video communicated was fear. Tom, you think you're doing God's will, but your motives are evil." I said, "If I were you, I'd burn that video."

Then I looked at Roger and said, "Roger, you don't have the Holy Spirit either because that was pretty low what you said last night about the Community castrating me. The Holy Spirit wouldn't say that." I looked at him and said, "My wife's been wanting me to talk to somebody for almost five years and I told her I would agree to talk to someone for a day. The way this was done this weekend was very sneaky. I was coming down here and I wasn't even aware of this meeting until I arrived at my wife's house. Neither she nor my father let on that this meeting was going to take place this weekend."

Tom said, "Oh, it had to be that way because if we had told you, you wouldn't have come, because your Community wouldn't have let you speak to us."

My wife said, "Oh, it won't happen again." She promised a couple of times that it wouldn't happen again.

On Saturday Tom had said that he had tried to talk to Yoneq and he had been given the run-around and no one knows where he is. I said, "But after listening to you Friday and Saturday, I'm not surprised if Yoneq doesn't want to talk to you." I told him, "I'm going to pray that our Father will have mercy on you because you're in a bad place." Not much more was said after that. I went outside with my children and we spent the last three hours together. We were out in the woods and when we came back Tom and Judy were gone, but Roger was still there. I left around 2:30.

About a week later I called my wife and asked her, "Could you give me Tom's last name because I want to write to him." She said, "His name is Bob Pardon." I said, "Wait a minute, I thought he said his name was Tom." She said, "No, he introduced himself as Bob." I said, "Tom and Bob — that's not even close." She said, "Well, when you were saying his name I was going to correct you, but I didn't."

I said, "If I had known that was Bob Pardon, that meeting probably wouldn't have gone as long as it did."

And she said, "Oh, that was God that allowed that."

—*Charles Beckwold*

THE QUEEN v. DAWSON

In January of 1988, Edward Dawson, known to his friends as Isaac, went to jail because he refused to tell the whereabouts of his four-year-old son Michael. Four months earlier, Family & Children's Services had seized his son in spite of a doctor's report that he had found no sign of abuse, either physical or emotional. Their grounds were based on a subjective opinion of the social workers in Nova Scotia, Canada, concerning child rearing and lifestyles. The Supreme Court of Nova Scotia eventually ruled in Isaac's favor — ten years later.

1998 — Looking Back

My name is Edward Dawson, but my friends call me Isaac. I am a member of a community of believers who lived in Nova Scotia from 1983 to 1993.[1] I haven't always lived in this community, so I would like to explain to you the events that led me to this new life and explain why I took such a drastic and all-out stand against the Department of Community

---

[1] This community relocated to Winnipeg, Manitoba, in 1993, where it remains today. Isaac now lives in a sister community in Nelson, British Columbia, which he helped establish.

Services, Family and Children's Services of King's County, and the Family Court when they took my son in September 1987.

I was born into the upper crust of the middle class, being the fourth child in a family of five. My parents provided well for us. I am appreciative of my parents for their care. As the years went by, I developed some serious attitude problems, which were most noticeable in school. I realized in elementary school that I wasn't cut out for this world and my behavior reflected it. My parents and teachers sought out remedies, but none were successful. I finally ended up in an English boarding school, which was good for a few years, but it was not the answer I needed.

At the age of eighteen, after a short stint in college, I decided to strike out on my own and see what the world held in store for me. I was the adventurous type, it was the early seventies, and the times were loose. People were "doing their own thing." Why not me? I decided to follow my heart, and things started happening for me.

My experiences took me from spending a couple of years on a privately sponsored sailing vessel visiting exotic locations and mixing with the who's who of the world, to gaining access to my own fortune through various business dealings and marriage to a wealthy young woman. I lived a life that most only dream about. I had become part of the ruling class. However, life at the top was lonely, and I felt that it was costing me my soul to maintain my position. One morning, I awoke to my screaming conscience, no longer able to live an empty life, prospering off the backs of others. Within a few months, I was divorced. My selfish life was starting to take its toll on me. I was lonely, alienated, and I felt disconnected.

Then it happened — the most fantastic event of my life. In January 1983, I became the father of a beautiful, blue-ribbon baby boy. My life took on new meaning. *For the first time there was someone whom I loved more than myself.* My son became everything to me. I took him wherever I went. I spent just about all my time with him. He was the center of my life.

I became preoccupied with his future. I had experienced the best that society had to offer, and it hadn't satisfied me. I knew it wouldn't do it for him either. Not only had my life not satisfied me, but I had been deeply damaged and hurt by my experiences. I could barely relate to my fellow man. My relationship with my parents and family was now almost nonexistent. I had some serious problems with women, and I could barely relate to even my male friends. I was alone, except for my new relationship with my son and a living arrangement with his mother. In reality, I had lived a selfish life, and the truth of it was that I needed help to find my way out, not only for myself, but also for my son.

I searched high and low. We lived in the country for a time, then back to the city. I knew it was more than geography. I was becoming desperate for answers. Who could show me the way? My son was becoming of school age, and he needed greater interaction with others. Who could I trust him with? I didn't trust anybody, either with my life or his. I needed *somebody* to trust!

It was at that point that I really began to think about God. Although I had not doubted His existence, I knew my life was far from what it was supposed to be. I knew deep in my conscience and spirit that I was falling short of the truth. It was time for a radical change. I began seeking the truth in any way I could. I started reading the Bible. I looked into the different churches, conventional and alternative. I asked the hard questions like, "What does it mean to *give up all your possessions?*" Nobody could answer me in a way that brought me peace.

In my search I came upon a community of people in Island Pond, Vermont. They had the life I desired for both my son and myself. In April 1986, I spent two weeks in the Community, visiting and observing the lives of these people. It was wonderful to see people so happy with so little. I could see there were still struggles in their lives, but unlike my struggles, they had answers and help from those around them. I saw fathers working with their sons, mothers with daughters, men and women living in harmony, men helping other men. It was beyond my wildest imagination. To this day, I sometimes still can't believe it is really happening.

I decided to become a part of this community, and because I was Canadian, I found my way to a sister community in Nova Scotia, Canada. Although it had been my desire to take my son and his mother with me, his mother chose to stay in Montreal and demanded that Michael remain with her. Although it was the hardest thing I had ever done, I left for Nova Scotia on my own. Within six months of my being in the community, my son Michael came to live with me. His mother was experiencing some instability in her life, and I was thrilled to have my son with me. He was four years old at the time.

I had finally found the life I had always wanted, and also a life for my son that would spare him from being the problem child that I had been. He was going to receive real help when he came to the hurdles in his life. He would face his problems and receive the correction at a young age so he wouldn't have to drag around his negative attitudes as I had all my life. His mother was satisfied about him being with me, and had signed a written agreement confirming my sole custody of him.

About nine months later, one fall day in 1987, two social workers and a Royal Canadian Mounted Police (RCMP) officer arrived at our community farm while Michael and I were on our way to feed the chickens. What was this all about? These social workers had a concern that my son was being abused, and they wanted to take him to a hospital for an examination. Having grown up in the society that I had, the only understanding I had of social workers was when they went on their fund-raising drives. They would never dare show their faces in my neighborhood for any other reason than to raise support.

I had no concept of the unlimited control and influence that they exercised in people's lives. I cooperated with their request after being assured that if there were no signs of abuse, then that would be the end of it. On the way to and from the hospital we discussed child-rearing methods. I openly told them that I spanked Michael when he needed it. They had a different opinion, but assured me that they would be satisfied with a favorable report from the doctor. There was no emotional or physical abuse found by the doctor when he examined Michael at the hospital, so he gave him a good report. We were returned to our home, believing it was over.

Several days later, I was served with a notice to appear in the Family Court. It turned out that the doctor had been given some newspaper articles about the community, and he had signed an affidavit written by a social worker reacting to those articles. The affidavit bore no relation to what the doctor had observed of my son or to the truth of our lives.

Working from the affidavit, the judge gave the local social services agency authority to investigate. The judge assured me that she just wanted "a window on our life" to make sure nothing was amiss. That "window" turned into a five-month ordeal that eventually took us to the Supreme Court of Nova Scotia. Ten years later, it continued all the way to the Supreme Court of Canada — and back.

During the course of the Family Court proceedings, one evening five police cruisers and no fewer than ten officers, accompanied by social workers, came to the farm to apprehend my then four-year-old son. Michael was helping with chores in the barn when they arrived. It was a scene I will never forget. Although I didn't resist the authorities, I could not consent to them taking my son either. The officers pleaded with me and tried to intimidate me. Michael was clinging to me with all his might. Two officers literally pried my son's hands from around my neck, ripping him off me as he screamed, "No! No! No!"

They lowered Michael into the back seat of one of the cruisers and whisked him off into the night with lights flashing. When asked, one of the social workers ashamedly acknowledged with a nod of her head that what was happening to my son at that very moment was clearly child abuse. But the officers were under orders — orders from the social workers. Our neighbors, a dentist, and high school French teacher, watched helplessly in utter disbelief.

Michael didn't see me or anybody else he knew until a higher court returned him to me 44 days later. He had been taken to numerous psychologists and was extensively grilled about my beliefs and the philosophy of our community. His foster mother kept copious notes on everything he did and said. It was almost as if they had captured an alien from another planet and wanted to know what made him tick. Michael held his own, and they were amazed at his loyalty. They called him, "brainwashed," yet gave totally favorable reports of his personality.

The social service personnel were indignant and bitter about the decision to let Michael go home, and immediately appealed to the Supreme Court of Nova Scotia. Meanwhile, as I continued on in the Family Court, the judge again ordered me to produce my son. I couldn't do it and didn't do it. I was jailed for contempt of court and ordered to stay in custody until I divulged his whereabouts. Twenty-six days later, after the appeal was heard, the Supreme Court of Nova Scotia released me and upheld the decision returning Michael to my custody. The Court said I should never have been found in contempt. We were elated. We thought it was over...

1988-1992 — Undoing the Damage

For the next few years, Michael and Isaac struggled to regain what had been stolen in that relationship. They made steady progress. Meanwhile, Isaac and his lawyer became actively involved in pleading for a new child protection law in Nova Scotia that gave proper respect to families and their right to stay together. Dawson traveled the province, meeting with parents, consulting with policy makers, and submitting his suggestions for changes to the law that allowed Michael to be so easily and so unjustly seized from him without cause.

He made numerous visits to Province House, the legislative assembly in Halifax, and told his story to the Law Amendments Committee. By September of 1991, three and a half years later, the new "Children and Family Services Act" became law. It enunciated parent's right to notice and a timely hearing where the government had to present evidence before breaking up a family. The government had responded, and many citizens expressed their gratitude. It had been time-consuming and self-sacrificing, but the effort was worth it. Dawson often assured his son Michael, "it would never happen again." Slowly, Michael regained his trust and his security that had been so rudely robbed.

The next chapter of this story began to unfold four years later...

Michael and Isaac Dawson - 1990

1992 — The Queen v. Dawson

On March 13, 1992, another sudden attempt was made to take Michael from me. Down the same driveway came a police car driven by an officer whom we all knew and liked. He handed me a stack of court documents. Once again, my son was on the line. Before I could even gather my thoughts, another car sped up the driveway. Michael's mother and her lawyer demanded Michael, insisting he go with them immediately. She had traveled over a thousand miles and hadn't told us she was coming. Her visits and phone calls had become sporadic and inconsistent over the last two years. She was making promises to visit and then not showing up, reflecting further signs of instability in her life.

Who had put her up to this? She had always been welcome to visit or stay anytime she wanted. Something was wrong. It turned out that a hearing had been held in the same Family Court earlier that week, without my being there. The court had issued an order for Michael's mother to have weekend access to him without my being informed or given a chance to be heard. I knew something was seriously wrong with how this visit had come down.

After consulting with my friends at the Myrtle Tree Farm and talking to my lawyer friend in Vermont, a fellow disciple, I agreed to allow supervised access, but not to let Michael out of my custody until I had the opportunity to be heard. Michael's mother refused the visit. Given everything that Michael had been through at the hands of the Family Court, I could not risk putting him through another ordeal like the first one. I did not go to court. I left the farm, knowing I was protecting Michael from an inevitable ordeal and imminent harm that he might never recover from. Within two weeks, Michael's mother had abduction charges laid against me.

On February 4, 1994, I was arrested by the FBI in California, where we had been living. Yet again, it happened without notice or hearing, and the authorities took my son. After a grueling two months in U.S. and Canadian jails, finally I was released on bail with conditions too detailed to mention, most significantly, that I could not contact Michael.

From the moment that our home in California was surrounded by numerous FBI agents, until my final acquittal, I was treated like a hardened criminal. When I was brought into custody, there were extra precautions taken in handling me. One of the guards, when he saw my paperwork, commented that I must have committed a very serious crime. What began as a simple access issue in a small rural town in Nova Scotia had turned into an all-out international manhunt, calling upon Interpol, the United Nations, and other private and governmental agencies in an effort to locate me — all this because I belonged to a community that the anti-cult movement considered threatening to mainstream society. Although, in 1988, Michael had been returned to me because there had been no evidence of any problem warranting state interference, there was no such happy result the second time.

Back in Nova Scotia in September of 1994, I was tried for abduction and *found innocent* by the court. The judge said I had lawful custody and possession of my son the whole time. I was so happy and so relieved! But within a few weeks time, again I was served papers. The Province of Nova Scotia had appealed my acquittal. Because of my bail conditions, I was confined to the province as I awaited the decision of the Nova Scotia Court of Appeals. I found myself without my community, my son, or my freedom, since the community had recently relocated to Winnipeg, Manitoba.

On July 5, 1995, in a decision from the Supreme Court of Nova Scotia, the court *reluctantly* ordered a retrial based on a technical point of law. Although Michael's mother and I had a written custody agreement, I was tried as if I did not even have custody, simply because no court had ever ordered it. However, there was a favorable dissenting opinion from one of the judges. He saw the reality that I had actual custody of Michael and said I could not be charged with abducting him. He also condemned the *ex parte* hearing in March 1992, because it denied me notice and the right to be heard in the first instance. Based on his opinion, I appealed that decision to the Supreme Court of Canada, as a matter of right.

During the time between my release from the bail conditions in October of 1995 and my appeal before the Supreme Court of Canada in June of 1996, I returned to a somewhat normal life in the Community in Winnipeg. During that time, the concerns of my heart continued towards my son's well-being. My contact with him was minimal, and he had been poisoned against my beliefs and my life, for his mother, all the while, was being greatly influenced by the anti-cult mindset against minority religions. Waiting for justice in the courts continued to take its toll on my ability to father my son.

As I sit here, I can't help but believe that tying up individuals in the court system is one of the anti-cult tactics in gaining control of people's lives. The time lost through this process is irreplaceable and only serves to widen the gap between those separated. It has become ever so clear to me what a vulnerable place children are in, influenced dramatically by those who are entrusted with their care. I often ask, "Where was the protection for Michael from the anti-religious philosophy that destroyed his moral character?"

In the decision reached by the seven judges from the Supreme Court of Canada on November 19, 1996, I was sent back to Nova Scotia for a retrial. Two dissenting judges, Justices McLachlin and Sopinka, found that the majority opinion was not worthy of Canada's constitution and its history.

Nearly a year later, on November 3, 1997, I returned to Nova Scotia where I represented myself in a two-week jury trial. The judge found in a pretrial hearing that my rights had been denied by private citizens who used "a certain degree of force to undermine this man's religion." These were Michael's mother, her lawyer, and a self-proclaimed "cult expert." Prejudicial evidence had been given at the *exparte* hearing in 1992 that had launched the initial access order.

At my trial I called the former director of the agency who had taken Michael without cause in 1987.

He candidly testified that, even though his workers had no evidence of abuse of Michael ten years earlier, they kept after us because they "weren't convinced there was no abuse." Upon this admission by agents of the province in front of the jury, the Crown Attorney stood up pounding the table, shouting "Alright! Alright! There was no abuse at the Myrtle Tree Farm!" I could almost say that was worth waiting ten years for the government to admit.

But my son's testimony was the highlight of the trial, when he testified about all that he had been through. He told the court that he knew that the reason I did what I did was to protect him from further harm. I was confirmed that his heart was still with me. There was also a great deal of testimony from others, members of my faith, related to the practices of the anti-cult influence in trying to separate their families. After almost two intense weeks in court, the jury found me *not guilty*. I was thankful for the final acquittal, but the cost in human terms had been high.

In reflecting on the last decade, I have asked many times, "Why did I have to defend myself, my son, my chosen life, and the community in which I live for ten long years?" It seems so unnecessary and unjust. Why couldn't it have ended sooner, before my son's life was destroyed?

One reason is that media reports of charges of child abuse in the Island Pond Community in Vermont — charges which they had been cleared of years earlier— were spread by newspapers and TV and by the Vermont S.R.S. and Social Services in

Nova Scotia. It has only been in the last few years that our community has come to understand that a network of so-called "cult" experts are committed to destroying groups who choose to live outside of the mainstream. It has become abundantly clear that there is a deliberate plan at work to incite government agencies, police authorities, and courts into actions that are neither based on truth nor founded in law. Often the actions that we have been accused of are the very actions that have been used against us — kidnapping, brainwashing, separating families, and outright child abuse.

It has been a long road, and my relationship with my son is almost completely destroyed. On May 10, 1998, my son was caught shoplifting a bottle of pop. The police returned him to his mother's apartment. They were extremely concerned with the condition of the apartment, it being unhealthy and unsuitable to live in. The whole environment Michael has been subjected to by his mother evidenced signs of mental and emotional distress. Based on their findings, they decided to take Michael into care.

Upon leaving the premises, they encountered his mother. She had been drinking alcohol and proceeded to tear into one of the officers, biting him on the arm while foaming at the mouth. This only confirmed the need to take Michael into care. She accused the authorities of being under the influence of "the cult," as she refers to us. It was clear from the police report that she is not fit to care for herself, let alone my son. This confirmed my worst fear — that the very mechanism that was designed to protect him ended up devouring him.

Michael is now desperately in need of my care and supervision, the love he has been deprived of when he most needed it. I can only hope and pray that it is not too late. "Love finds a way" is the path I believe in... I grope to find that path with Michael. He is abused, but this abuse has been at the hands of those who abused both him and me, and it is the influence of an anti-cult agenda that has no concern for truth, or rights, or children. Fortunately, my faith has seen me through these trials.

The times we live in are not easy. At the appeal of my acquittal, my lawyer told the court, "If Isaac Dawson were not a member of the Myrtle Tree Farm Community, I do not believe he would even be charged." I believe that to be the truth. At this time in history, it seems to me that with the future of humankind in such question, there might be some room for individuals to seek the truth:

> *"From one man He made every nation of man, that they should inhabit the whole earth; and He determined the times set for them and the exact places where they should live. God did this so that men would seek Him and perhaps reach out to Him and find Him, though He is not far from each of us." (Acts 17:26-27)*

What Happened to Michael's Best Interest?

Years after Dawson's initial arrest, tapes of that 1992 hearing revealed, once again, that the judge and the investigating RCMP officer had been influenced and persuaded by untruthful testimony by so-called cult experts about Dawson and his faith. In the absence of evidence, action was taken, contrary to principles of fundamental justice, that continue to have its damaging effects on the lives of Michael Dawson and his father.

The next section expresses Edward Dawson's reflections of the past decade, looking back, wondering how all this could have happened, and looking forward, hoping his son can recover and come home:

For the last ten years of my life, I have been caught up in a relationship with the powers of the state that I would like all who value the concept of freedom of religion to be aware of. As a human being born into a middle-class life in the free world, I was always under the impression that I would be free to live my life according to my beliefs. Since then, I have learned otherwise through first-hand experience. Freedom to live and act according to my religious convictions, and having those convictions protected under the law, may be just a concept. The very freedom that I needed to be protected — freedom to live outside the mainstream of today's decadent society— cost me ten years of my life. I am willing to pay the price, but the real question is, "Can my son recover from the damage he has borne at the hands of irresponsible government?"

As I sit here, I can tell you that my encounter with the powers of the state in my well-documented case of *The Queen v. Dawson* has left me numb. The relationship between a human being and his family, and the delicate balance that exists in the family, is not something to be tampered with by any governmental agency.

Throughout the years, as my integrity was brought under scrutiny in regard to my ability to father my son, there was a recurring theme. It had little to do with my heart towards caring for my son, but exposed the greater scheme to try and separate me from my faith. The end result was to undermine my relationship with my son and my inalienable right to direct the affairs of my household. The concern was not for the "best interests of my son" as it was so often labeled, but more what was perceived as the best interests of society as a whole, as judged by those who disregard basic human rights. The authorities, in their continued efforts to invade beyond their reasonably justified authority in my life, exemplified an aspect of government that continually needs to be kept in check by men of conscience, if there is to be any hope in the 21st century to avoid the bloodshed and oppression of the past.

I was continually amazed by the unrelenting efforts of the state in their attempt to have me surrender to them, beyond the sphere of authority that has been given to those who administer the affairs of government. At every turn, I strained to listen to my human spirit in responding to their requests. It was always clear to me what to do. When it came to the areas where the state had authority,

I submitted. When they were encroaching on my inalienable rights, I had to take a stand, or else my human voice would have been silenced. I would have become a lowly worm of a man.

In many ways, that may be part of what perpetuated such a lengthy ordeal. I came to see that when the state was flexing its authority, it was powerful and unbending, but when a court decision exonerated me, there was no sign of yielding by the state, right to the bitter end, and no responsibility taken for its wrongful actions.

In the early stages of its investigation, there was room for some degree of error in the state's ignorance, given the somewhat alternative nature of my life. For example, I choose to home educate my son within my community. It seems to me that the authority of state needs to be satisfied that children are being taken care of according to the personal preferences of the individuals, but not to dictate how.

In the early stages of my encounter with the state, I made every attempt to accommodate their requests. However, once the highest authority in the province had rendered a decision, finding that, beyond my lifestyle and all the lies and accusations that were leveled against myself and the community, there was nothing to "justify the terrible sanction of separating the boy from his father." At that point, I felt that it would be over, but that was not to be the case.

The need to justify the system became of greater importance than to preserve the very purpose government was created — to punish evil and to reward good. Individuals within the different government agencies and others within the court system had received unsubstantiated, inaccurate reports about me and my community, and they were now committed to proving them.

At the conclusion of the last trial, the final battle in this ten-year war, I stood before a four-woman, eight-man jury. After two weeks of pouring out everything humanly possible in a court geared to law, I knew my only hope for victory was in the conscience of the jurors to do the right thing. Throughout the trial, there was no indication of how they would rule. However, I knew that in their hearts lay the decision of whether I was innocent or guilty.

Throughout this ten-year period, as my life was handled by the myriad of individuals from social workers, administrators, court clerks, jailers, guards, and policemen, to the over twenty judges, in over fifty or more days in court it was their instinctive, inborn ability to judge between what was right or wrong that made the difference.

For those who did the right thing, there was peace; for those who didn't, there was chaos and confusion, and ultimately havoc in my son's and my life. As I stood waiting for the jury foreman to proclaim the final verdict, my fate once again lay in the conscience of these individuals. I could barely respond to the "NOT GUILTY" judgment. There was no satisfaction or glory in that moment, only a certain comfort in knowing that they had done the right thing. Almost in the same moment, the Crown prosecutor turned on his heels, grabbed my hand, and congratulated me, wishing me a good life.

Only moments before, he had accused me of being a "threat to society," having been the last of a long list of individuals "just doing his job."

I now realize from my broken life the only hope that will allow a new and lasting social order to come about is that there would be individuals in positions of authority who would stand for justice and make righteous judgments, committed to following their conscience — not merely their own opinions, imposed on others. I appreciate those public servants who did just that.

—Isaac Dawson

DAVID SAYLOR'S KIDNAPPING

Could it be? Has it been 25 years, one quarter of a century? The full-colored images are still so clearly etched in my mind. The vivid details remind me of that dramatic three-day encounter. The indelible imprint on my soul surprises me, surfacing just last week during the most unrelated activity you could imagine. My youngest son (who just turned 15) and I were catching chickens. There were so many of those white chickens, clucking and fluttering on the floor of the dimly lit wooden barn. I purposely stayed close to the two-hinged doors where a sunbeam streamed through a narrow crack. I became aware of the chicken farmer's conversation with his wife. The hot-flushed feeling was coming back, dreaded but familiar. "John, I think we need to darken the barn if we want to catch these chickens," she suggested. He moved toward the door and fastened it securely with the rope that hung from the nearby hook.

The door was shut, the sunbeam had vanished, and darkness all around had engulfed me. I tried to inhale, but unsuccessfully, tingling sensations racing up my paralyzed spine. The door, the escape route — where was it? It was so hot, the pit of my stomach burned deep inside me. The moment in time focused — this split second of time seemed to expand and magnify as I stood there. "Dad? Dad?" It was my son's voice, "Dad, can you hold this side of my crate?" Reality returned, and my frame quivered as I stooped to grasp one side of the heavy crate. The doors swung open and I welcomed in the chill wind as it blew against my face. We swung the crate up together to the waiting truck.

The surrounding details vary depending on the circumstance, but the scenario remains consistent. For years, even living in the loving environment of the Community, I refused to even look into what caused those moments of panic and terrifying feelings of claustrophobia. But in the more recent months I am finding myself able to verbalize my feelings as I see a familiar recurring pattern. This intensely uncomfortable panic visits me when in the dentist's chair, my mouth full of dental equipment. At other times, I may be sitting in a wooden chair in a room full of people and suddenly notice that the door is three rows away from me.

Curiously enough, I never encountered this phobia previous to the attempt my relatives made to dissuade us from becoming immersed in the life of the Twelve Tribes, a community of believers that was then dwelling in Northern Vermont. Under the persuasion of cult awareness "authorities," our families felt compelled to "rescue" us by means of "de-programming" from the certain danger they believed would come upon us if we were to carry out our heart's desire to become one with the group of people we had found, sharing a common life in the quaint village of Island Pond.

In the first moments of the kidnapping that took place to bring about their plan, I struggled with my two brothers-in-law. It was then that I felt as if a venomous poison was being injected into my soul. We were all young, strong men back then, but I was no match for my wife's brother, a trained RCMP officer. I felt myself overcome by their strength, as a strong arm held my head and shoulders tightly locked. I was closed in, and there was no escape, nowhere to go, no air to breathe.

I nevertheless continued resisting as I was forced into the back seat of the waiting car. My father behind the wheel, we turned into the city boulevard, and hope sprang up in me as I spotted a city police car in the next lane. In one last desperate attempt I called out, "Help, help, I'm being kidnapped!" I screamed. The window went up and the police car continued on, unaware of my plight. I sank into the back seat, defeated, helpless.

This violent scene has found a recessed corner of my soul and hides there; but much like a dormant volcano, the venom will erupt and spill over me at those unexpected moments — a very dark, suffocating sensation.

To help you understand our story, I want to give you a picture of how my wife and I arrived at the decision to make this drastic change in our lives. I say *drastic* because in our lives we were very comfortable and had what many only dream of. We had a cozy little brick bungalow situated in a Montreal suburb close to the airport. My two little girls enjoyed presenting me with flowers when I would come home after a long day of flying across the continent as a pilot in an Air Canada DC-9. In a few months my wife would be delivering our third child. In spite of all this, there was emptiness, a longing that our affluent life did not seem to be filling.

We began to tell our families of the life we were observing among these amazing people in Island Pond. So why, our families wondered, just at this time when everything appeared to be going so well, would we throw it all away to live in a community?

We continued to visit back and forth with our new friends from Island Pond. We were guests in their homes, and some of them came up to Montreal to stay with us on business trips or just for social times. We asked lots of questions, watched mothers with their children, and even learned a few songs. We were unmistakably drawn to them and began to realize that the love and care they had was what we lacked in our own lives. Somehow a little house and well-paying jobs (my wife had been an RN) with all the material comfort to go along with it began to be empty and lifeless to me in comparison with what these people had.

We continued to speak to our families and friends about what we were seeing and experiencing, and received many different responses. A growing quietness was happening. They didn't want to visit

Island Pond, and they didn't respond as we were responding. The communication between us became strained and awkward on all sides, and you could feel the tension mounting.

My wife's older sister and her husband, both good friends of my wife's and mine, came to visit with us during that time. Strange things began to happen. During their visit, I arrived home from a flight, and as I turned a corner, I met my brother-in-law. "Strange," I thought out loud, "That you would come to town and us not know about it."

Then a phone call came from another brother-in-law asking us come to a meeting with him and some other people he'd invited. My wife asked him to come to our house instead, and he declined. Shortly after that, two cars pulled up in our driveway containing my father, my wife's father, her sister, a close friend, and the two brothers. The house was now full with family members in an unexpected family reunion, but it was certainly not anything like our usual relaxed congenial family holidays.

Something was wrong. We could sense an eerie feeling in the living room. Then came the beginnings of what in only a few moments would become the only violent experience we have ever had. With quick motions, one of my wife's sisters bundled up my sleeping son, someone else was putting my two daughters in a car, and my wife was told, "Come with us, Karin. We already have the three children." Maybe it was during this time that her arms and legs got bruised.

I felt myself spinning around, what is going on? A dark suffocating sensation engulfed me. I was being forcibly dragged or maybe pushed out the door. This is the recurring fear that comes to me in the chicken barn or amidst a room full of people. It is amazing to me how a few minutes in time so many years ago can still have such an impact on my responses.

The drive up to the Laurentien Mountains lasted for about an hour, and during that time it began to dawn on me what was happening. Our families had just kidnapped us! Being early April, the ski season was over for the winter, making available a chalet to be rented for the purpose of deprogramming us. My parents and my wife's parents were in a little cabin across the parking lot, and all the rest of us seemed to be in this two-storey frame house.

It was amazing how many people were cooperating with this plan. A good friend of my wife's had agreed to come along in the capacity of caring for our three children during the sessions. This woman was a registered nurse with experience in pediatrics, and had a friendship with my daughters. The two grandmothers were busy in the kitchenette preparing a snack, and greeted us as we entered the house. Also present were the four deprogrammers — Naomi Goss and her husband Barry, along with two other women from Florida.

The front entrance opened up to the house's living room, with a television near the front and a fold-up table behind the couches. On the table were several stacks of papers. Up the stairs was a bathroom and bedrooms, one of which we were to share with my wife's sister and her husband.

The next morning we — my wife and children with some of our family — walked out in the parking lot and by a little brook. Upon returning to the house Naomi clearly stated that should not happen again, and that we should not leave the house at all. The family complied with her wishes, and the doors were locked from then on. Over the period of the next three days a strange course of events unfolded. The house at most times contained the nineteen people involved, and during the sessions our family members were right there with us, hearing what the deprogrammers had to say, and watching the videos. This information was affecting them and us at the same time. We watched videos depicting the Nazi regimen, with Adolph Hitler training his troops, and also the approach on life of the Hare Krishna's and the followers of Sun Myung Moon was presented.

Leading questions with fore-gone conclusions were asked. One discussion was related to the type of food provided for members of this "cult." We explained how when we were weekend guests we were served breakfast one morning that consisted of eggs and toast. Naomi responded with, "Yes, as long as you're a guest you will get eggs and toast, but after you join they'll make you eat oatmeal."

My wife and I burst into laughter at that point because oatmeal "porridge" was what her father had delighted in cooking for many of their family breakfasts when they were growing up. But somehow the way Naomi said it there was now something wrong with having oatmeal for breakfast.

The children in Island Pond were being described as malnourished, deprived, and mistreated physically and emotionally. I knew Naomi had once lived in the Community, so upon asking her why she had left, she replied, "I left because they wouldn't let me get braces on my teeth." This, of course, implied that dental care didn't exist for the children. But this didn't make sense to me, because on my visits to Island Pond, I saw children wearing braces. Where were their "facts" coming from?

The strain on all of us was becoming evident with the passing hours. My wife overheard one of the deprogrammers talking to her sister, telling her how they keep watching the person's responses for a phenomenon to happen. The person being deprogrammed will come to a snapping point, when they emotionally collapse, signaling a successful deprogramming session. So my wife and I decided to look for an opportunity to cause them to think this had happened to us. On the third day, a movie was being shown on the television. A group of shivering children was lined up along a bleak cement wall, having cold water poured on them from a garden hose. The scene looked pathetic. At this point my wife began crying hysterically. Her sister, beside her on the sofa, put her arms around Karin to console her. "Now will you listen to us?" And Karin sobbed even louder. From the back of the room someone said, "That's it, she's snapped!"

"That's good! Now we can go on to the second phase. What's next is a rehabilitating environment, like a half-way house." Naomi began to explain how we would now be taken to another location for a period of time necessary to re-integrate us back into normal society.

My wife and I went to the bathroom and looked at one another, "Oh no," she whispered, "It's not over. Just another plan. What are we going to do? How can we get out of here?" We were very disturbed and rattled. You could sense a very powerful force at work. We returned to the living room, but shortly afterwards I told my wife, "It's enough. We're going to bed."

Our families were totally affected by all the information being presented, and all the implications, especially the insinuations of child abuse. But they were becoming confused because we were showing the allegations as untrue through our responses. What we had seen happen during our time visiting in Island Pond was not consistent with the accusations from Naomi and Barry. Tension was growing and growing.

It was around 11 p.m. as we headed up the stairs to bed. On the way, Karin's younger brother stopped her. "Just tell me the truth," he said, "and I'll believe you. Do they beat their children in Island Pond?"

"No," was her reply.

He then determined to bring this thing to a close. After talking at length with the others, Karin's brother made a decision. He was on his way up to our room to *get us out of there*. The RCMP brother stopped him on the stairs. They disagreed on how to handle things and a wrestling match started. Pandemonium hit. The deprogrammers knew it was over. From upstairs in our room we heard noises and the front door slammed. Someone ran off into the darkness. Then my wife's sister and her husband followed. She was only wearing socks and a thin windbreaker, unaware of the freezing temperatures outside. We got up quickly and went down stairs. In Barry and Naomi's room, all that remained to be seen were the swinging clothes hangers in the closet. My parents had quickly sped away to the US border to deliver the deprogrammers safely on the other side.

The next morning, after a long night, we made attempts to pick up the broken pieces. My brother-in-law and I decided to go and look for his brother and sister and her husband, who had been the ones who had left on foot. I don't think I will ever forget the picture of my father-in-law sitting on a small stool in the center of the living room in the chalet. He watched in amazement as the RCMP brother and I went to search for the family members who had fled the house. He sat there, slumped over, and as he spoke, tears filled his eyes. He quietly said, "I don't understand. We came here to help you, and now it's you helping us."

There are so many details of this experience that are not known to us. I have often wondered about the financial difficulties this must have brought on our families. Our families are hard-working, conscientious people, but not considered wealthy. The four deprogrammers were paid their wages, which

I had heard was several thousand dollars. Airline tickets, food, and lodging in a ski chalet quickly add up, as do bills for renting vehicles and taking time from work. We know this came from our family's pockets. They made their decisions to embark on this deprogramming based on information they'd received, believing it to be in our best interests, attempting to save us from impending harm. The long hours and years of suffering that have followed result from the lies they had been told.

Now that I can identify and write these things, I am beginning to be able to control these overpowering feelings. Yet, even greater than the suffocating effects on my own soul are the long lasting effects that the powerful and subtle lies of the cult-awareness "experts" have had in our personal family relationships. I know my parents, how they think and respond in situations. It was not their normal response. They raised me and passed on to me who they were, but under this powerful network of cult-awareness experts, the lies became influencing factors that began to dictate their choices. They loved us and became afraid for our well-being, so they acted impulsively. But their well-meaning intentions became twisted into something else by the involvement of the cult-awareness counselors. This is evidenced by the fruit of this attempted deprogramming. There remains, 25 years later, alienation, hard feelings, estrangements, bitterness, and mistrust.

My own father devoted much time to studying cult groups and gathering information for years afterward. Our relationship was never able to be healed past the point of social politeness. One day I called him and he let me know he was experiencing health problems. He was curious about my daughter's upcoming marriage to one of the young men here. Curiously, he remarked, "I don't understand some things, but I'd like to." These were his last words to me. The next day his life ended.

I sincerely hope that this article will help you to understand the danger of believing hearsay over personal experience. You may be a parent, with your child becoming interested in the Twelve Tribes, and you may need to come to peace about his or her decision. Or you may just feel the need to understand. Please feel free to call us. Even if you would like to personally call me at home, I would be glad to talk with you. My wife and I don't want others to experience the devastation that took place in our families.

— David Saylor

MY VERY OWN "CULT SCARE"

A PUBLIC DEFENDER'S OBSERVATIONS

In a few short years, about half of my life will have been spent learning first-hand about the anti-cult movement and the current colloquial trends surrounding the use of the word "cult" to describe varied and diversified new religious movements. Let me just say, every step along the way was worth it to know what I know now.

In 1983, when I was 32, I was a public defender in northeastern Vermont who was assigned to represent a so-called cult member accused of simple assault for a supposedly vicious beating of a pre-teen girl. The details of the charge were particularly horrific,[1] so

---

[1] I have written extensively about this case and the details can be found elsewhere. "The Twelve Tribes Communities, The Anti-Cult Movement and Governmental Response," Jean Swantko, in *Regulating Religion: Case Studies from Around the Globe*, James Richardson, Ed., Plenum Publishing (2000) pp.185-186. See *www.twelvetribes.org*, search "Wiseman case".

much so that I almost refused the case, thinking that my emotions would be too affected to give my client the legal representation that he deserved. The local and statewide press at that time was replete with scandalous, inflammatory, and defamatory publicity both about him personally and also his church group, referred to then and there as the Northeast Kingdom Community Church.[2]

After much soul-searching and heartfelt discussion with my partner at the time, I concluded that "everyone deserves a vigorous defense, even if he is accused of something awful, so I am at least going to meet this fellow. I will handle the case unless I no longer can, due to my own conscience." And that was how it all began. Every step along the way I determined to follow my own heart, despite both predictable and surprising pulls in opposing directions.

First off, when I met my client in mid-August 1983, I was impressed by his composure and his faith. He was not abnormal, remote, or beady-eyed. He looked me straight in the eye, answered my direct questions, and did not exhibit any strange auras. A couple of months later I took him up on his offer for me to visit his church group, the Community in Island Pond. When I decided to attend a church wedding, I was taken aback by the apprehension and fear my colleagues and friends had for my safety, as if I might be entering an unknown "Twilight Zone" with a distinct possibility that I might not return the

---

[2] Over the past 35 years, the international group now known as the Twelve Tribes Communities has been known by different names since its inception in 1972: the Vine House, the Light Brigade, the Northeast Kingdom Community Church, the Church in Island Pond, Vermont.

same as they had known me, or even that I might not return at all.

But, quite the contrary, I had an exceptionally good time, both surprising and alluring. There were several hundred people — joyful men, women, and children — singing, dancing, and showering their love on the couple being married. It was a Friday. My client was not present, but as it happened the leader of the group was in attendance, just returning from a trip. Someone introduced me to him, and, lo and behold, he spent a lot of time with me, personally explaining the significance of all that was happening. All of it was fascinating to me, intriguing, enlightening and meaningful, but not the least bit strange or off-putting. I drove home that evening very excited about what I had just encountered, convinced in my own heart that I had not witnessed abused children or abusing parents, which was the main charge against the group at the time. It was just not believable.

But what began to work inside me was a question that only grew more gnawing as the months passed: Why was this group so controversial, and who was it that was against them?

An early experience that invoked my intuition occurred when I returned to work that Monday and the local daily paper was sitting on my desk. There I was, in a large picture on the front page! It was a photo of Gene Spriggs and me talking. I was unnamed, but my colleague had drawn in a cloud over Spriggs, saying "Cult Leader!" I was mildly shocked and somewhat amused. The significance of my visit eluded me, but somehow there was a reporter present from a statewide newspaper who captured the moment. In the ensuing months "covering the cult" became his obsession. What consumed me was my desire to understand all the hype and the hysteria. Everyone in my office was curious to hear about my visit. Questions abounded.

Over the next year my boyfriend and I visited the community often, usually on Sundays when everyone gathered for a big celebration. We were welcomed, our many questions were answered, and we were more and more intrigued by what we saw. At the same time, negative press coverage only escalated, and it was the Attorney General's office that handled the case, rather than the local county prosecutor. Momentum against the group was gaining and some of my friends were becoming distant.

As I became more involved with the case, I awaited the deposition (questioning under oath) of the alleged victim with anticipation. I knew her demeanor and her answers would reveal a lot. I had determined that my client would be present. I wanted to observe her in his presence. But when the day came, her father objected in every way. "No way is my daughter going sit across the table from him!" he exclaimed. The state lawyer pleaded with me to remove my client. "It's his constitutional right to be there and he's not giving it up." I retorted. Both men were present. As I asked the questions, observed the girl, and heard her answers, one thing became crystal clear to me: the girl was not afraid of my client. It was obvious that she considered him her friend, confirming exactly what he had told me.[3]

Somewhere along the way I saw the need for my client to speak for himself in court. He was articulate, knew what needed to be said, and it was his faith at stake, not mine. We decided to ask the judge whether we could be co-counsel, and the judge granted our request. Not long after, at a hearing about "excessive pre-trial publicity," my client called me as a witness, a somewhat unorthodox move. There was a different judge that day and he did not like what was happening. He warned me that my client would be giving up his attorney-client privilege if we proceeded this way. My client spoke up and said "That's alright, Your Honor. I have nothing to hide." The point that he drew out of me was that I, too, had been afraid and skeptical of his church group until I had visited for myself. "Why?" he asked me. "Because of all the lies that I read in the newspaper! Until I could see for myself, I believed them — or at least I was affected by them." I said unequivocally.

As the case meandered through the court for two years, my relationship with the church community grew. I got to know many members individually, learning what drew them to the group. One thing I concluded early on was that it was clear that each one of them served the same God, despite diverse backgrounds, income levels, and educational achievement. I was also exposed to many teachings and gatherings. All I knew was that the group had

---

[3] For an account of how this girl's father was used by the anti-cult movement, see the 1998 Affidavit of Roland Church at *www.twelvetribes. org.*

life and that they loved each other with a pure heart. The more I got to know them, the stranger it seemed to me that there was such a furor over these people. What was going on behind the scenes that I was unaware of?

I just went forward one step at a time, following my heart and my instincts. I decided to depose the Attorney General himself, as he had said in a radio broadcast that he was "confident of a conviction" in my client's case. Now this is something that prosecutors are not supposed to do, comment on a pending case, as it violates ethical canons. He was obviously uncomfortable and fidgety. He didn't really know anything about the group, but it was as if he was "on a mission."

In due time the charges against my client were dismissed. The state police lost a key tape that they should not have lost, and the prosecutor was found guilty of an ethical violation for pursuing a conviction rather than the evidence. It was June 1985.

Meanwhile, I was still getting to know the little church community that lived as the Bible described in the Book of Acts (chapters 2 & 4). One evening about a year earlier, I was visiting the community and was invited to spend the night. It was already dark, my boyfriend was on a hiking trip, and it seemed like a good idea. I stayed up late talking with two of the women, and then went to bed in a room by myself. The next thing I knew it was 6:45 the next morning and a state trooper with a big hat and a long, huge flashlight burst into my room and pointed its glare right at my face. He said "Get up, get dressed, we're here to take the children!"

It was Friday, June 22, 1984. Ninety Vermont State troopers in bulletproof vests and fifty social workers raided nineteen homes in the pre-dawn hour, demanding the names of the children and the children themselves. They waved papers as if they had a flag of victory demonstrating the State's conquest over the religious beliefs of the individuals involved. A local judge had signed a search warrant to legitimize the roundup of the unsuspecting children, so the zeal of the social workers became unleashed to confidently intrude into the lives of these little ones as if they were doing them a great favor, rescuing them from the abusive clutches of their fanatical parents. 112 children were unlawfully seized that morning because of the religious beliefs of their parents.

We were transported, in custody, to the courthouse in Newport, Vermont, some 20 miles away, where each family awaited its turn to appear before a judge who would decide whether they would be separated or kept together. Happily for the parents, Judge Frank Mahady was a man who respected the State Constitution of Vermont as well as the U.S. Constitution, and who did not judge by the barometer of public opinion. As he properly called the lawyers from the State Attorney General's Office to provide evidence of abuse to justify the seizure of each child, the State of Vermont was left with nothing to say, except to speak against the faith of those brought to court.

Court continued late into the night, calling each child by name. Each one was sent home with his parents, as there was no basis to keep even one for examination by the state's battery of doctors, social workers, and psychiatrists who sat to no avail nearly an hour away at a ski resort, waiting to perform their scrutinizing rituals. At around 9 pm, Judge Mahady had to decide what to do with the large group of children, approximately sixty, whose parents would not give their names, despite the coercion of law enforcement's threatening tactics. After hearing the arguments, he released them *all* to return home with their parents. He gave the opportunity for any parent who had something to say to speak. Many passionately told the story of their day and spoke of their deep gratitude for a judge who ruled justly. By 11 pm, a bus of tired, but rejoicing families headed home to Island Pond, singing the praises of their God and giving thanks for the judge whose humble response was, "I'm only doing my job."

I was thankful to have been an eyewitness to the State of Vermont's "grossly unlawful, unconstitutional scheme"[4] to destroy the Church in Island Pond. Although I already knew that something was very, very wrong, it was not until fifteen years later that it could be proven that there had been a deliberate plan afoot to destroy the little group. It was written, six pages long, and conceived by a mercenary anti-cult zealot named Galen Kelly for the price of $1000. He devised it at the request of Priscilla Coates, then director of the Cult Awareness Network. The two had visited the

---

[4] Swantko, Jean, *supra* at f.n. 1; video entitled "*The Children of the Island Pond Raid: An Emerging Culture,*" 2004, *www.twelvetribes.org*

Attorney General's office in Vermont on August 9, 1983, and persuaded the state government to execute the steps of the plan. It did so meticulously. They had actually deceived government officials to simply go along with their plot, such was the powerful effect of their lies, their tactics, and their agenda.

The faith of community members and their trust in their God prevailed. A decent judge who practiced according to the Constitution was placed on the bench that day. He saw clearly the unlawfulness of the scheme and the targeting of people based on their religious association.[4] But no one knew back then that it was not simply the result of inadvertent good intentions. I knew it in my spirit, but the facts and the evidence to prove it were elusive and remote, taking time, diligence, attentiveness and divine intervention to accumulate.

Nevertheless, I was drawn to the spirit of the group, their love for each other, and their God. In September 1985, I left my former life behind and joined the Community Church in Island Pond. Over the years, the missing pieces of the puzzle surfaced to reveal a hateful and malicious scheme to destroy the group.

The anti-cult movement is alive and well around the globe, on its mission to squelch religious freedom by promoting fear of new and different religions, as if individuals are not entitled to "grope for God." The bad press and lies from Vermont in the early '80s has circulated to Canada, Europe, and Australia, influencing governments, anti-religious "sect commissions," and individuals, to the detriment of the truth.

The anti-cult movement is calculating and deceptive, with intentions to plant fear and use scare tactics through the media to execute plans to destroy small groups. It is worldwide in scope, and its nature is to accuse, to point the finger. Evidence is not necessary. They can manufacture it somehow. It is the nature of the evil one to accuse. As the world careens toward the brink of destruction, the eternal battle between good and evil dominates the world stage. No one can deny that it is getting worse and worse. As for me, I am thankful that I could find out for myself what the truth was and follow it, and not to be deceived by the lies and tactics of the anti-cult movement. I hope for you that you will not be taken in by their lies.

—Jean Swantko Wiseman

WHY TO BE SCARED OF THE ANTI-CULT MOVEMENT

The following is an excerpt from "The Twelve Tribes Communities, The Anti-Cult Movement and Governmental Response" Social Justice Research Journal, *12 (4), 2000, pp. 360-361. The complete article is available at www.twelvetribes.org.*

The anti-cult movement has been referred to as an *industry* by scholars.[1,2] It is not a reliable source when seeking the truth about the Twelve Tribes. After decades of harassment by the anti-cult movement (henceforth referred to as *ACM*), a review of the Twelve Tribes' legal history[3] reveals that anti-religionists have repeatedly influenced governments to unfairly prosecute or adjudicate controversies surrounding members of this religious minority.

---

[1] Shupe, Anson (1998) "The Role of Apostates in the North American Anti-Cult Movement" in *The Politics of Religious Apostasy,* D. Bromley, Ed., pp.209, 212-213, Westport, CT, Praeger

[2] Palmer, S.J. (1998) "Apostates and Their Role in the Construction of Grievance Claims against the Northeast Kingdom Community Church" in the *Politics of Religious Apostasy, Ibid.* at p.198

[3] See Swantko, "The Twelve Tribes Communites, The Anti-Cult Movement and Governmental Response," see footnote 1.

Religious discrimination by the government becomes apparent when one studies the facts and sees that, in case after case, anti-cult data was not a trustworthy source to rely on before making official judgments and taking public action.

The agenda of the former ACM-oriented Cult Awareness Network includes activities that have been well-documented. The following list, derived from a careful reading of James Lewis[4] suggests a pattern of action that seems demonstrated by the experience of the Twelve Tribes Communities around the world. The steps include:

(1) ACM representatives, including deprogrammers, contact disaffected ex-members (who may be engaged in a custody dispute);

(2) they coordinate ex-members' meeting with media representatives to stir up public opinion;

(3) after sufficient concern is aroused in the general public, they arrange for ex-members to give affidavits about abuse of some sort to social workers to begin regulatory and court proceedings;

(4) they use courts, sometimes in *ex parte* (one-sided) hearings, to get judgments against the group that might eventually cause great harm to the organization;

(5) they used the exaggerated and even untrue information to further promote the ACM agenda, which in turn causes more people to seek their services (which may be expensive); and

(6) then they use this information to raise funds from the public to help fight the "cult menace."

---

[4] Lewis, J.(1994) From The Ashes, Lanham, MD, Rowman and Littlefield.

All of these methods have been demonstrated by the ACM industry's effort to destroy the Twelve Tribes' Communities.

In the face of such tactics, Twelve Tribes' members eventually have been vindicated time and time again in the courts, although not without considerable disruption and difficulties for members. Prosecutors and local law enforcement and social services workers entrusted to promote the public good repeatedly relied on untrustworthy ant-cult information, which resulted in an abuse of state authority directed toward Twelve Tribes' Communities.

The ACM destroys the delicate balance that maintains social and political order by breaking down the boundaries of rightful authority separating government and religion. This is especially a problem in societies such as France and Germany, where there is a close relationship between private anti-cult groups and the government.[5] By effectively influencing governments to believe that certain religious groups are a social menace because of what they believe, the stage is set to pursue individual members on a selective basis because of their "dangerous" faith, without reliable evidence that criminal or anti-social activity has happened.

The law, in some countries, prohibits accusing someone based on guilt by association because guilt is personal, not communal.[6]

---

[5] See articles by Massimo Introvigne and Hubert Seiwert in *Social Justice Research Journal*, (Vol. 12, No. 4, 2000), see footnote 1.

[6] *Scales v. U.S.*, 367 U.S. 203, 224-25 (1961)

The ACM thrives in the gap, created by a failure in both governments and religions to recognize the legitimate authority of the other and to properly define their own social and political boundaries. Governments have been deceived into police action by emotional misrepresentations, persuaded to believe them and trust that force is necessary to maintain the public welfare. Anti-cultists, sometimes motivated by religious orthodoxy or anti-religious sentiment instead of religious liberty, have sought to limit religious diversity, and cry "heresy!" or "abuse!" to provoke government interference in areas in which the government should not tread.

The ACM takes advantage of both mainstream religions and insecure government officials by invoking fear and inducing "moral panic" [7,8] in the public arena. The result is to convince governments that true religious diversity is unnecessary, and at the same time to convince established religions that anything outside the mainstream is dangerous and deserves to be destroyed. This trend is happening now and it is escalating around the world. To maintain a democratic social order, it is essential that false information, induced hysteria and fear do not replace vigilant, conscientious and effective law enforcement and government policies.

If you value freedom and democracy, you are justified to be scared of the anti-cult movement.

* * * * *

[7] Goode, E. & Ben-Yehuda, N. (1994) *Moral Panics: the Social Construction of Deviance*, Cambridge, MA: Blackwell

[8] Introvigne, M. (1990), *Freedom of religion in Europe and the question of new religious movements* (presented at CESNUR Conference, Torino, Italy).

THE TWELVE TRIBES COMMUNITIES

Since our humble beginnings in Chattanooga, Tennessee in the early 1970s', the Twelve Tribes Communities have spread to nine countries on four continents with nearly fifty communites. Through many opportunities and great opposition, we are begining to emerge as a brand new culture as our successive generations continue what was in the hearts of their parents — to see God's Kingdom come on the earth, just as it is in Heaven. We welcome anyone who is interested to learn more about us to visit any one of our communities or cafes listed below:

UNITED STATES (1-888-893-5838)

TENNESSEE
Community in Chattanooga
900 Oak Street, Chattanooga, TN 37403 ☎ (423) 752-3071

The Yellow Deli
737 McCallie Avenue,
Chattanooga, TN 37403 ☎ (423) 386-5210

Community in Pulaski
219 S. Third St., Pulaski, TN 38478 ☎ (931) 363-8586

Common Ground Bakery at the Heritage House
219 S. Third St. Pulaski, TN 38478 ☎ (931) 363-8586

VIRGINIA

Community in Hillsboro *(Washington, DC area)*
15255 Ashbury Church Rd, Hillsboro, VA 20132
☎ (540) 668-7123

NORTH CAROLINA
Community in Asheville
9 Lora Lane, Asheville, NC 28803 ☎ (828) 274-8747

Community Conference Center *[between Statesville and Taylorsville]*
471 Sulphur Springs Road, Hiddenite, NC 28636 ☎ (828) 352-9200

GEORGIA

Community in Brunswick
927 Union Street, Brunswick, GA 31520 ☎ (912) 267-4700

Common Ground Bakery
801 Egmont St. Brunswick, GA 31520 ☎ (912) 264-5116

Community in Savannah
223 E. Gwinnett St, Savannah, GA 31401 ☎ (912) 232-1165

FLORIDA

Community in Ft Myers
2706 First St., Fort Myers, FL 33916 ☎ (239) 337-3472

VERMONT

Community in Island Pond
P. O. Box 449, Island Pond, VT 05846 ☎ (802) 723-9708

Simon the Tanner - Family Outfitters
Cross & Main Streets, Island Pond, VT 05846 ☎ (802) 723-4426

Basin Farm
P. O. Box 108, Bellows Falls, VT 05101 ☎ (802) 463-9264

Community in Rutland
134 Church Street, Rutland, VT 05701 ☎ (802) 773-3764

Back Home Again Café & Hostel
23 Center St, Rutland, VT 05701 ☎ (802) 775-9800

MASSACHUSETTS

Community in Boston
92 Melville Ave, Dorchester, MA 02124 ☎ (617) 282-9876

Common Ground Café
Dorchester Ave, Dorchester, MA 02124 ☎ (617) 298-1020

Community in Hyannis
14 Main Street, Hyannis, MA 02601 ☎ (508) 790-0555

Common Ground Café
420 Main St., Hyannis, MA 02601 ☎ (508) 778-8390

Community in Plymouth
35 Warren Ave, Plymouth, MA 02360 ☎ (508) 747-5338

Common Sense Wholesome Food Market
53 Main St Plymouth, MA 02360 ☎ (508) 732-0427

NEW HAMPSHIRE

Community in Lancaster
12 High Street, Lancaster, NH 03584 ☎ (603) 788-4376

NEW YORK

Community in Coxsackie
5 Mansion St., Coxsackie, NY 12051 ☎ (518) 731-7711

Simon the Tanner - Family Outfitters
7 Mansion St, Coxsackie, NY 12051 ☎ (518) 731-2519

Oak Hill Plantation
7871 State Route 81, Oak Hill, NY 12460 ☎ (518) 239-8148

Oak Hill Kitchen
7771 State Route 81, Oak Hill , NY 12460 ☎ (518) 239-4240

Common Sense Farm
41 N. Union Street, Cambridge, NY 12816 ☎ (518) 677-5880

Common Ground Café & Bakery
10 E. Main St. Cambridge, NY 12816 ☎ (518) 677-2360

Community in Oneonta
81 Chestnut Street, Oneonta, NY 13820 ☎ (607) 267-4062

Common Ground Café
136 Main Street, Oneonta, NY 13820 ☎ (607) 267-4062

Community in Ithaca
119 Third Street, Ithaca, NY 14850 ☎ (607) 272-6915

Maté Factor Café
143 East State St, Ithaca, NY 14850 ☎ (607) 256-2056

Community in Bethel
177 Perry Rd, Cochecton, NY 12726 ☎ (845) 583-1071

MISSOURI

Community on the Lake of the Ozarks
1130 Lay Ave, Warsaw, MO 65355 ☎ (660) 438-4481

Common Ground Café
145 Main Street, Warsaw, MO 65355 ☎ (660) 438-2541

Stepping Stone Farm
Rt. 2, Box 55, Weaubleau, MO 65774 ☎ (417) 428-3251

Common Ground Café
100 W. Hwy 54, Weaubleau, MO 65774 ☎ (417) 428-0248

COLORADO

Community in Manitou Springs
41 Lincoln Ave, Manitou Springs, CO 80829 ☎ (719) 573-1907

Maté Factor Café
966 Manitou Ave, Manitou Springs, CO 80829 ☎ (719) 685-3235

CALIFORNIA

Community in Vista
2683 Foothill Drive, Vista, CA 92084 ☎ (760) 295-3852

The Yellow Deli
315 Main Street, Vista, CA 92084 ☎ (760) 631-1833

Morning Star Ranch
12458 Keys Creek Rd, Valley Center, CA 92082 ☎ (760) 742-8953

CANADA (1-888-893-5838)

Community in Winnipeg
89 East Gate, Winnipeg, Manitoba R3C2C2, Canada ☎ (204) 786-8787

Common Ground Café
79 Sherbrook St Winnipeg, MB R3C2B2, Canada ☎ (204) 453-5156

Community in Courtenay
596 Fifth St, Courtenay , BC V9N1K3, Canada ☎ (250) 897-1111

Mount Sentinel Farm
2915 Highway 3a, South Slocan, (Nelson), British Columbia V1L4E2, Canada ☎ (250) 354-2786

Preserved Seed Café
202 Vernon St, Nelson, BC V1L4E2, Canada (250) 352-0325

Fair Field Farm
11450 McSween Rd, Chilliwack, BC V2P 6H5 Canada ☎ (604) 795-6199

The Preserved Seed Cafe'
45859 Yale Road, Chilliwack, BC V2P 2N6 ☎ (604) 702-4442

The Community in Vancouver
4261 Marguerite St., Vancouver, BC V6J 4G2 ☎ (604) 733-6416

GERMANY

Gemeinschaft in Klosterzimmern
Klosterzimmern 1, 86738 Deiningen, Germany ☎ (49) 9081-290-1062

Prinz & Bettler Café
Reimlinger Straße 9 Nördlingen, Germany ☎ (49) 9081-275-0440

ENGLAND (0800-0743267)

Stentwood Farm
Dunkeswell, Honiton, Devon EX14 4RW, England ☎ (44) 1823-681155

SPAIN

Comunidad de San Sebastián
Paseo de Ulia 375, 20013 San Sebastián, Spain ☎ (34) 943-32-79-83

Sentido Común
General Echagüe 6, 20013 San Sebastian, Spain ☎ (34) 943-433-103

Comunidad de Nerja
Balcón de Europa 5 B, Nerja, Malaga Spain, ☎ (34) 952-527054

Little Flock Café
Balcón de Europa 5 B, Nerja, Malaga, Spain ☎ (34) 952-527054

FRANCE

Communauté de Sus
11 route du Haut Béarn, 64190 Sus/Navarrenx, France
☎ (33) 559-66-1428

Communauté de Heimsbrunn
71 rue de Galfingue, 68990 Heimsbrunn, France ☎ (33) 389-819-300

ARGENTINA

Comunidad de Buenos Aires
Batallón Norte y Mansilla 120, 1748 General Rodriguez, Buenos Aires,
Argentina ☎ (54) 237- 484-3409

BRAZIL

Comunidade de Londrina
Rua Jayme Americano 420, Jardim California, 86040-030 Londrina,
Paraná, Brazil ☎ (55) 43-3326-9664

Comunidade de Campo Largo
Caixa Postal 1056, 83601-980 Campo Largo
Paraná, Brazil ☎ (55) 41-3555-2393

Café Chão Comum
Rodovia do Café BR 376, KM 297, 86828-000 Mauá da Serra,
Paraná, Brazil ☎ (55) 43-8812-2280

AUSTRALIA

Community in Sydney
3 Calderwood Road, Galston, NSW 2159, Australia ☎ (61) 02 96533953

Common Ground Café
586 Darling St, Rozelle, NSW 2039, Australia ☎ (61) 02-9555-6369

Peppercorn Creek Farm
1375 Remembrance Dr., Picton, NSW 2571, Australia
☎ (61) 02-4677-2668

Common Ground Café in Katoomba
45 Waratah St, Katoomba, NSW 2780, Australia
☎ (61) 02-4782-9744

Call us toll-free 24 hours a day:
1-888-TWELVE-T
1-888-893-5838
or visit our web site at:
www.twelvetribes.org